☑ **W9-BGB-790**

Baseball Cards
Questions & Answers

Edited by
Mark K. Larson

Published by
Krause Publications Inc.
700 E. State St.
Iola, Wis. 54990
Telephone: (715) 445-2214

INTERNATIONAL STANDARD BOOK NUMBER: 0-87341-216-8
LIBRARY OF CONGRESS CATALOG NUMBER: 90-60580

Printed in the United States of America

Contents

Introduction 3

1. General Information
History & Terminology 4

2. Card Grading & Taking Care of Your Cards
Learn To Do It Right! 29

3. Card Identifications
Including Scarce Issues 48

4. The Five Ws of Baseball Cards
Who, What, Why, Where & When 99

5. Factors Relating to Card Values
What Makes Cards Worth Money 133

6. Buying, Selling & Trading Cards
Get The Inside Track 157

7. Errors & Variations
Miscues Lure Collectors 165

8. Reprints, Collectors' Issues & Counterfeits
Know The Difference 197

9. Collecting Autographs
The Rights & Wrongs 207

10. Baseball Memorabilia
A Diverse Field 221

11. Investing in Baseball Cards
Make Cards Work For You! 258

- 1992 Cards 269

Introduction

When he was just a kid, Leonard Garcia, through a first-hand experience, probably had some of his questions about baseball card collecting answered. Garcia, a batboy for the California Angels, became an integral part in Topps' baseball card production for 1969. The youngster conspired with Angels' third baseman Aurelio Rodriquez and fooled Topps' photographer into taking his picture for a baseball card instead of the Angel infielder's. Yes, that's Garcia with a mischievous smile pictured on card #653 in the 1969 Topps set.

So, how much is that card worth? How is its value determined? The updated, expanded second edition of **Baseball Cards Questions & Answers** provides answers to those ques-

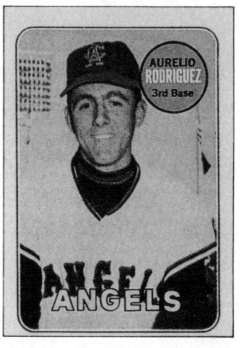

tions and more, covering the ins and outs of baseball card collecting from start to finish from when the photographer takes a player's picture for a card, to when the finished product ends up in the hands of a youngster opening a new wax pack of cards. It's designed to offer both beginners and advanced collectors, the primary audience, answers to often-asked questions regarding all areas of card collecting and memorabilia, and introduces them to a base of information which can be used in building, enhancing, and enjoying their collections. The history and terminology of this nostalgic, fun and profitable hobby is traced, and all its aspects are discussed. Plus, there are hundreds of photographs which accompany the text.

This hobby exploded in the 1980s. National baseball card shows are drawing more than 25,000 people, and some card prices continue to rise toward levels of small real estate figures. The hobby is becoming more sophisticated, and there's more to keep tabs on to stay on top of the hobby. **Baseball Cards Questions & Answers** offers a more-than-elementary look at carefully-selected questions which those who are entering this exciting hobby may have regarding collecting in the 1990s.

General Information

Chapter One

What makes baseball cards collectible?

There are several reasons baseball cards are collectible. One major reason is the nostalgic aspect of cards. Like old Wurlitzer juke boxes and decoder rings, baseball cards often serve as a happy reminder of our youth. The surge in value and investment potential for baseball cards in the last 10 years has also drawn many people to the hobby. In 1989, a top grade 1909 T-206 Honus Wagner sold at an auction for $115,000. In a 1991 auction, hockey star Wayne Gretzky and Los Angeles Kings owner Bruce McNall paid $451,000 for a Mint T-206 Honus Wagner. A more recent card, the 1952 Topps Mickey Mantle, has rocketed from about $1,000 in the early 1980s, to $3,300 in 1987, to $8,900 in 1990, to $20,000 in 1992. Collectors also see baseball cards as objects of art, collectible on their artistic merits. The popularity of the game of baseball also adds to the collectibility of cards and related memorabilia.

How long have people collected baseball cards?

People have collected baseball cards since they were first produced in the 1880s. Kids have always swapped cards with their friends, but collecting didn't begin in earnest until the 1970s. A small gathering of 13 West Coast collectors in 1969 is generally regarded as the first organized baseball card show. By the time the group met in 1973, it needed accommodations for 650.

That rapid growth rate held true for the entire country in the 1970s and 1980s. A recent West Coast show, for instance, attracted more than 30,000 enthusiastic collectors, while more than 70,000 collectors attended the 12th National Sports Collectors Convention in Anaheim, Calif., July 4-7, 1991. Today, the baseball card hobby still draws thousands of new participants annually and shows no sign of letting up.

How many people collect baseball cards?

Serious collectors number anywhere from 500,000 to more than a million or more. But the number of people who collect baseball cards, casually and seriously, is nearly three million and growing rapidly.

When was the first baseball card made?

The first nationally-distributed baseball cards were issued by Goodwin & Co. in 1887. The 1½" by 2½" cards featured posed studio photographs glued to stiff cardboard. They were inserted into packages of cigarettes with such exotic names as Old Judge, Gypsy Queen and Dogs Head. The poses were formal, with artificial backgrounds and bare-handed players fielding bags on strings to simulate action.

What is a tobacco ' card?

From the late 1880s to the early-1910s, baseball cards were inserted into tobacco products to stimulate sales, thus the name "tobacco" cards. From 1887-1896, several sets were issued. But by the mid-1890s, the American Tobacco Co. dominated the cigarette market, so there was no reason to issue baseball cards and the company phased them out. But in the years prior to 1910, the threat of Turkish tobacco imports spurred domestic companies to reintroduce baseball cards as a way to bolster sagging sales.

From 1909-1912, dozens of different sets were produced. Among them were the extremely popular 1½" by 2⅝" color lithographed set of more than 500 players, which collectors call the T-206 set, and the 5" by 8" Turkey Red brand card set, also known as the T-3 set. Also produced were double-folders, featuring two players on one card, and triple-folders, featuring two player portraits and an action scene. Gold ink and embossed designs were also used as companies vied to make their cards more attractive and popular.

This era of card manufacturing saw the issue of the "king" of baseball cards, the 1909 T-206 Honus Wagner card. It is estimated that about 50 of these cards exist today.

General Information

What's the real story behind the T-206 Wagner card?

Wagner reportedly opposed cigarette smoking, so he wished his likeness would not be used to endorse cigarettes. Thus, the card was pulled from circulation, accounting for its scarcity. It's more likely Wagner objected because he was not paid royalties by the tobacco company for the use of his picture, so he insisted the card be pulled.

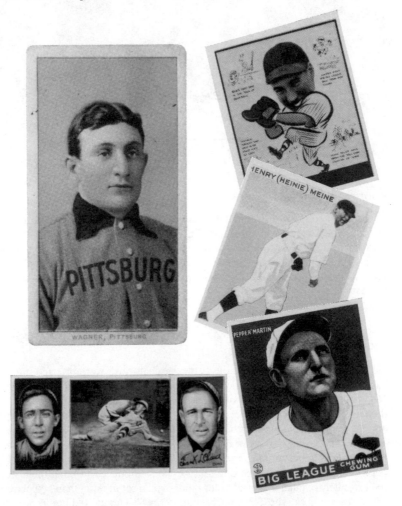

When were bubble gum and baseball cards first sold together?

Though often referred to as "bubble gum cards," it's been just more than 50 years since gum and cards teamed up. It was in the 1930s when rubber tree products were used to give gum the elasticity needed to blow bubbles. The National Chicle Co. and Goudey Gum Co. were major card producers in the 1930s. The companies sold a slab of gum and one card in a colorful wrapper for one

cent. Most of the cards measured 2½" by 2½", and the players were depicted in colorful paintings. In 1939, Gum Inc. entered the market, becoming the major card producer until the outbreak of World War II. No cards were produced from 1941-1948. Wartime shortages required a pooling of all national resources, including paper and ink, for the war effort. Baseball card production resumed after the war and hasn't stopped since.

What kinds of products have been sold with baseball cards?

From the 1910s on, baseball cards have been issued with such diverse products as caramel, chocolate, cookies, Cracker Jacks, magazines, ice cream, milk, soft drinks, tea, meat products, dog food, potato chips, cereal, Jell-0, beef jerky, snack cakes and macaroni.

General Information

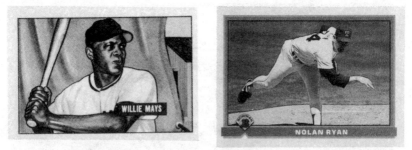

How come Bowman is making cards again? Didn't this company stop making cards in 1955?

The Bowman Gum Co., formerly known as Gum Inc., produced baseball card sets from 1948-1955. In 1951, Topps began producing baseball cards. During the next five years, the two companies competed, until in 1956, when Topps bought out its competitor. Topps again released sets of cards in 1989-1991, using the Bowman name.

Why is Topps known as "The Real One?"

"The Real One" is the Topps slogan which bears some truth. Topps has issued baseball cards since 1951, longer than any card company, and held a virtual monopoly on the baseball card market from the time it bought out Bowman until 1981. In 1981, when a federal court smashed Topps' monopoly on the issuance of cards with bubble gum, the Fleer Corp. and the Donruss Co. broke into the market. Although a later court decision cost the upstart companies the right to include bubble gum with their cards, the companies stayed in the market. Since then, three other companies have entered the card industry: Sportflics in 1986; Score in 1988; and Upper Deck in 1989.

What makes baseball cards valuable? Also, why are rookie cards so expensive?

Like any other collectible, a baseball card's value depends on market demand. A card's condition, its scarcity, and, in some cases, its age are important factors. Outweighing all other considerations, though, is demand. When the chips are down, a card is "worth" whatever the buyer is willing to spend to own it. Rookie cards, or the first cards issued for a player that depict him as a major leaguer, are the hottest segment in the hobby today. One reason they are valuable is because collector demand has caused rookie card prices to rise significantly in recent years. In 1992, a 1968 Topps Nolan Ryan rookie was valued at $1,200; a 1967 Topps Rod Carew rookie was at $475; a 1955 Topps Roberto Clemente rookie was at $1,500; and a 1975 Topps Robin Yount rookie was at $225. Collectors buy rookie cards much in the same manner book collectors buy first editions of books. Rookie cards should not be confused with what collectors call "pre-rookie" cards, which are cards of minor league players.

8

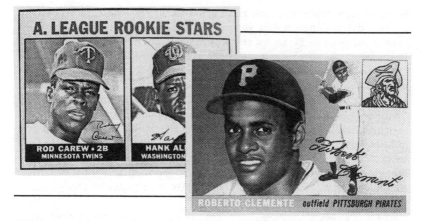

Are baseball cards a good investment?

All signs say baseball cards are still a very sound investment. A recent article in *Money* magazine rated baseball cards among the best investments of the 1980s.

The number of convention attendees increases every year, as do the circulations of leading baseball card periodicals. That means more people are catching the baseball card bug, which in turn means prices for older cards should continue to rise also.

Every year, more and more collectors clamour for a finite supply of baseball cards. The demand is increasing, while the supply, obviously, cannot. In most cases, the money a collector puts into a baseball card will yield a hefty return just by virtue of increasing demand. More detailed information regarding investing in cards is located in the "Investing in Baseball Cards" section of this book.

Is there a standard grading guide for cards?

Yes. *Sports Collectors Digest* and *Baseball Cards* magazine originally formulated a set of grading standards for the hobby in 1981. Since then, the *Sports Collectors Digest* and *Baseball Cards* staffs have refined those standards. Howeveer, these grading standards are flexible; all collectors and dealers are always free to judge any specimen according to their own tastes and collecting standards. A detailed grading guide, accompanied by terminologies and illustrations, is located in the "Card Grading & Taking Care of Your Cards" section of this book.

Is there a price guide available for baseball cards?

Many price guides have appeared in the past 30 years. For instance, Jefferson Burdick's 1960 reference work, *The American Card Catalog*, attempted to provide collectors their first reliable gauge of a constantly fluctuating market.

The problem with most price guides is that they age quickly. The baseball card market changes rapidly, so last year's price guide will be outdated rapidly, too. For example, Burdick's *Catalog* can only reflect a 1960 economy in its prices. Outdated 1960 prices are no help to the contemporary collector in today's frenetic market. Each year, to help collectors keep up with the baseball card market, Krause Publications, of Iola, Wis., publishes *Sports Collectors Digest Baseball Card Price Guide,* a definitive book-length guide to more than 80,000 cards and related baseball memorabilia. Throughout the year, the same publisher furnishes a monthly price guide magazine, *Sports Card Price Guide Monthly,* to keep collectors even more informed of price changes as they occur. Krause also publishes pricing information weekly in *Sports Collectors Digest.* For the collectors' convenience, these annual, monthly and weekly price guides list card values in several card conditions.

Where can I buy, sell and trade baseball cards?

Collectors buy, sell and trade baseball cards from other collectors, at baseball card shops, shows and through the mail, and from advertisements in baseball card books and periodicals. For more information and advice, consult the "Buying, Selling & Trading Cards" section of this book.

I want to start a baseball card collection, but with so many cards, I don't know which ones to collect.

There are many baseball cards in the marketplace today. A frequent mistake made by new collectors is to buy everything in sight. But by doing this, you may be left with a hodgepodge of cards rather than a collection. For the beginner, the main thing to remember is to define the focus of the collection. Find out what cards you like, and don't feel pressured to buy every card available.

Buying complete regular issue sets from the major card companies is a popular form of collecting. The attraction of having a complete set from a company such as Topps or Fleer is that it includes the cards of nearly every major leaguer who played that year.

Many collectors focus on a specific team or player, such as collecting all the cards relating to the Boston Red Sox or Hank Aaron. The areas of collecting are limited only by your mind. Some collectors specialize in autographed cards, superstar or rookie cards, power hitters, players of a particular position (center fielder, shortstop, etc.), ugly players, MVP winners, no-hit pitchers, or players from their home town or state — the list could go on and on.

General Information

Another collector avenue is minor league sets, which feature players who have not broken into the big leagues. Collectors can follow these "unknown" players from their first years in the low minors right into the majors.

A newer collecting pursuit is unopened card packs. While most card packs are opened right after they're bought, some collectors save them in unopened condition. Years later, after a majority of the packs have been opened, these collectors still have cards in original packs. And since the top and bottom cards of some packs are visible, collectors seek those with star players such as Don Mattingly showing.

Are football, basketball and hockey cards collectible?

They sure are. Although baseball cards are the most popular among collectors, the number of football, basketball and hockey card collectors is growing rapidly. Also, "non-sport" cards, or cards that portray subjects other than sports (such as television shows or movies), are collectible.

What's the best way to display and store my collection?

A popular way to display a collection is to place cards into multi-pocketed plastic sheets which can be placed in a three-ring binder. By doing this, you can view many cards with less risk of damaging them. As for safe and clean storage, specially-designed card boxes and individual card sleeves are a wise purchase. These fairly inexpensive supplies are available through hobby dealers who advertise in established hobby periodicals such as *Sports Collectors Digest* and *Card News*. Some of these items have even made their way into retail stores. Turn to the "Card Grading & Taking Care of Your Cards" section in this book for detailed information.

Common Terms & Definitions

Airbrushing — An artist's technique used on baseball cards in which logos on uniforms or hats are altered or eliminated. Baseball card companies use airbrushing to depict a player with his current team if they do not have a photo showing him with that team.

All-Star card (AS) — A card which denotes a player's selection to the previous year's All-Star team.

ACC — *American Card Catalog.*

Autographed card — A card which was personally autographed by the player depicted. Cards with facsimile signatures, printed on many cards as part of the design, are not considered autographed cards.

Autograph guest — A current or former player or other celebrity who attends a card convention to sign autographs for fans. A fee, which can range from a few dollars to more than $30 for a player such as Joe DiMaggio, is usually charged for the autograph.

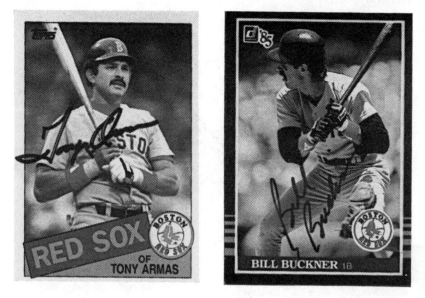

Baseball's Best — A set made by Donruss in 1988 and 1989. Also the name of a boxed set made by Fleer in 1987 and 1988, and the name of the set of insert cards made by Baseball Cards magazine in 1989 and 1990.

Bazooka cards — Cards issued with boxes of Bazooka Bubble Gum (1959-1971, 1988-1989).

Big cards — The trade name for Topps' oversized, glossy-finish card issues produced from 1988-1990. The cards are reminiscent of Topps' cards from the 1950s.

Blank backs — A card that has a blank card back. Most collectors feel these cards are merely damaged, with a lower value than correctly-printed specimens. However, some collectors will pay premiums for superstars or rookies.

Blanket — An early 20th-century collectible consisting of a square piece of felt or other fabric depicting a baseball player. Most popular are the 5" by 5" B-18 "blankets" from 1914, so-called because they were sometimes sewn together to form a blanket.

Blister pack — A blister pack is a method of card packaging in which cards are packaged in hard plastic on a cardboard backing, with three or four pockets of cards. Issued by Donruss (1987-present).

Borders — The portion of a card which surrounds the picture. They are usually white, but are sometimes other colors. Border condition is very important to the card's grade and value.

Bowman (B) — A baseball card manufacturer (1948-1955) bought out by Topps in 1956. Topps has issued sets under the Bowman name from 1989-91.

Boxed sets — These are sets produced by one of the major card companies, usually in conjunction with a business, such as K-Mart or Walgreens. Boxed sets usually contain less than 60 cards, most of which are star players. The sets retail for $2-$4.

Box panel cards — Bonus cards which are featured on a panel of wax boxes of the major card companies. Donruss originated the idea in 1985. Complete sets range in size from four to 16 cards, and feature superstar or star players.

Brick — A "brick" of cards is any grouping of cards with similar characteristics, such as a 100-card brick of 1975 Topps cards. Bricks usually contain common cards.

Buy price — The price a dealer is willing to pay for cards or memorabilia.

Buger King cards (BK) — Cards issued in conjunction with Burger King (1977-1987).

Cabinet card — A large card from the 19th or early 20th centuries, usually issued on heavy cardboard.

Card lot — A "lot" of cards is the same card, such as a 1988 Topps Don Mattingly card, sold in a lot or "grouping" of five, 10, 25, 50, 100 or whatever number of cards. A collector purchasing a "lot" of cards gets the cards at a discounted price, as opposed to buying a single card. Example: a single Mattingly card costs $1, but 100 Mattingly cards cost $75, or 75 cents each.

Case — A sealed case containing wax boxes or other product units which card companies sell at wholesale to dealers or retail stores. For instance, a 1990 Topps "wax case" is made up of 20 "wax boxes."

Cello pack — A package of about 30 cards wrapped in a printed cellophane wrapper that allows you to see the top and bottom cards. There are usually

General Information

24 cello packs to a cello box, and 16 cello boxes to a cello case. Cello packs retail between 70 and 80 cents. Issued by Topps, Fleer and Donruss.

Checklist (CL) — A list of every card in a particular set, usually with space allowing the collector to mark whether he has the card. A checklist can appear on a card, in a book or elsewhere.

Cal Ripken, Jr.

Rickey Henderson

Classic cards — Baseball cards made by Game Time Ltd., to go with its "Classic Baseball" trivia game (1987-present).

Coin — Can refer to an actual coin struck to commemorate an achievement made by a team or player; also, a collectible made from or with a combination of plastic, paper or metal, issued as a set, such as the 1988 Topps Coin set.

Collation — The act of putting cards in order, by hand or machine, usually numerically.

Collector issue — A set of cards produced primarily to be sold to collectors and not issued as a premium to be given away or sold with a commercial product.

Common card — A card which carries no premium value in a set. "Common" is a blunt way of saying the player depicted is not a star.

Condition — (See section on "Card Grading & Taking Care of Your Cards.")

Convention — Also known as a baseball card show or trading card show. A gathering of anywhere from one to 600 or more card dealers at a single location (convention center, hotel, school auditoriums or gymnasiums) for the purpose of buying, selling or trading cards. A convention is open to the public, and often times a fee is required to attend the show. Many conventions feature a player or several players to sign autographs.

Counterfeit cards — Cards made to look like original cards, and distributed with the intention of fooling a buyer. High-demand cards are the most likely to be counterfeited.

CY — Cy Young Award.

Dealer — A person who buys, sells and trades baseball cards and other memorabilia for profit. A dealer may be full time, part time, own a shop, operate a mail-order business from his home, deal at baseball card shows on weekends, or any combination of the above.

Die-cut card — A baseball card in which the player's outline has been partially separated from the background, enabling the card to be folded into a "stand-up" figure. Die-cut cards that have never been folded are worth more to collectors.

Disc — A circular-shaped card.

Donruss (D) — Baseball card manufacturer (1981-present).

Donruss Rookies (DR) — A 56-card post-season set issued by Donruss which includes rookie players (1986-present). Sold exclusively through hobby dealers in a separate box.

Double print (DP) — A card printed twice on the same sheet, making it twice as common as other cards on the sheet. Topps double-printed cards in virtually every set from 1952 to 1981. This was done to accommodate the year's set size on standard company printing sheets.

Drakes — Ohio-based bakery which made baseball cards in the 1950s, and again from 1981-1988.

Error — An error is usually found on card backs in the statistical or personal information, and sometimes on the card front (such as a reversed negative). If an error is not corrected, the error adds nothing to the value of the card. If the error is corrected, it is called a "variation" card.

Exhibit card — Postcard-size cards which pictured baseball players and other celebrities. Exhibit cards were produced from the 1920s-1960s, and were sold in penny arcade machines.

Factory set (F or FAC) — A complete set collated (packaged) by the card-producing company. Issued by all companies.

First card (FC) — Price guide designation which refers to the first appearance of a player in the major card sets.

Fleer (F) — Baseball card manufacturer (1959-1963, 1981-present).

Fleer Glossy Tin (FG) — Limited-edition set produced by Fleer, which features the year's regular issue set in a high gloss finish and is sold in a tin box (1987-present). Fleer Update sets are also done in glossy style.

General Information

Fleer Update (FU) — A 132-card post-season set from Fleer which includes players traded to other teams during the season, and rookies (1984-present). Sold exclusively through hobby dealers in its own separate box.

Food issue — A set of baseball cards or related memorabilia which was issued in conjunction with a food product, such as Post cereal or Hostess snack cakes.

Gallery of Champions — The trade name for a set of metallic reproductions of Topps cards made and sold by Topps from 1986-1988. The metals used included bronze, aluminum, pewter and silver.

Goudey — Baseball card manufacturer (1933-1936, 1938, 1941).

Grades — The physical state or condition of a card. (See section on "Card Grading & Taking Care of Your Cards" for detailed information.)

Hand collated set (H or HC) — A complete set put together by hand using cards from wax, cello, rack or vending boxes.

High-numbers — A term used to describe the final series in a particular set of cards. "High numbers" were generally produced in smaller quantities than other series and are, therefore, scarcer and more valuable.

Hall of Famer (HOFer) — A card picturing a member of the Baseball Hall of Fame, in Cooperstown, N.Y. Hall of Famer cards almost always command a premium over other cards.

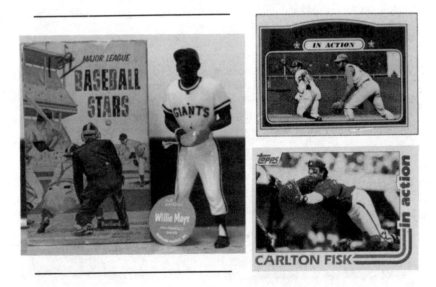

Hartland statues — A Wisconsin plastics company which produced, among other things, statues of baseball players in the late 1950s and early 1960s. The company reproduced the set in 1989 as Hartland's 25th Anniversary Commemorative Edition. Original statues are highly collectible.

In Action card (IA) — A card featuring a star player, designated with the words "In Action" on the card front. Most notably from the 1972 and 1982 Topps sets.

Inserts — A collectible included inside a regular pack of baseball cards to boost sales. Inserts have included posters, coins, stamps, tatoos, special cards, etc.

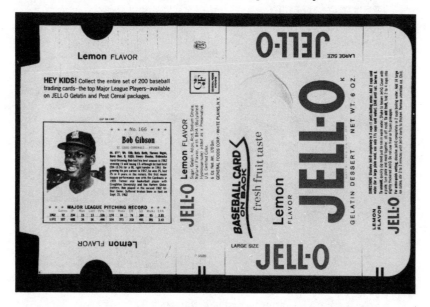

Jell-O cards — Cards sold as premiums with Jell-O packages (1962-1963).

Kellogg's cards — Simulated three-dimensional cards given away in cereal boxes or via a mail-in offer (1970-1983).

Key cards — The most important (valuable) cards in a set, such as the Mickey Mantle card, a "key" card in the 1952 Topps set.

Last card — The final regular card issued for a player; Hank Aaron's "last" card was in the 1976 Topps set. No particular extra value is added for last cards.

Leaf-Donruss — Baseball cards produced by Donruss specifically for the Canadian market (1985-1988, 1991).

Legitimate issue — A card set issued as a premium with a commerical product to increase sales; not a "collector issue."

Letter of authenticity — A letter stating that a certain piece of memorabilia, such as a uniform, is authentic.

Lithograph — A high-quality art print made in limited quantities.

MVP — Most Valuable Player award winner.

Mail-bid auction — An auction where bids are sent through the mail, with the highest bidder winning the merchandise.

Major set — A large, nationally-distributed set produced by a major card manufacturer, such as Topps, Fleer, Donruss, Score, Sportflics or Upper Deck.

Megalot — A megalot describes a group of cards, usually 1,000 or more of the samc player, purchased for investment or speculation.

Memorabilia — Refers to items other than cards, such as uniforms, bats, autographed baseballs, magazines, scorecards, pins, statues and the like.

Minis — Cards which resemble the regular issue cards in every way, except they are smaller in size. Most notable are the 1975 Topps Minis.

Minor league cards — A card depicting a player from the minor leagues. Minor league sets are a fast-growing segment of the hobby.

Mother's Cookies cards — An Oakland, (Calif.)-based cookie company which produces popular, high-quality glossy-finish regional sets (1982-present).

Multi-player card — A card picturing more than one player.

Non-sport card — A trading card or bubble gum card picturing a subject besides sports. Non-sports cards have depicted movie stars, television shows, mo-

ments in history and other topics.

Obverse — The front of the card displaying the picture.

O-Pee-Chee (OPC) — A Canadian card producing company (1965-present). O-Pee-Chee is Topps' official Canadian licensee, and O-Pee-Chee cards are almost identical to Topps' issues of the same year.

Panel — A strip of two or more uncut cards. Some card sets are issued in "panels."

Phone auction — An auction where bids for baseball cards or other memorabilia are taken over the phone. The highest bidder gets the merchandise.

Plastic sheet — A polyethelyne or polyvinyl sheet designed to store baseball cards, the most common being the nine-pocket sheet (which fits today's standard-sized cards). The sheets have prepunched holes on the left side which allows them to be placed in a three-ring binder.

Play Ball — The name of baseball cards produced by Gum Inc. (1939-1941).

Police/Fire/Safety sets — Card sets sponsored by public law enforcement or fire fighting agencies and a major or minor league team. Card backs usually contain anti-drug messages, fire prevention tips or other safety messages.

Post cards — Cards sold as premiums on or in boxes of Post cereal (1960-1963, 1990-1991).

Pre-rookie card — The name given to a major league player's minor league cards.

Price guide — A periodical or book which contains checklists of cards, sets and other memorabilia and their values in varying conditions.

Price on request (POR) — A dealer will advertise a card P.O.R. if he believes the card will fluctuate in price from the time he places his ad until the time the ad is seen by the public.

General Information

Promotional cards — Cards produced by the card companies which serve as a marketing tool for their upcoming cards. Promotional or "promo" cards are often sent to dealers to entice them to order cards. Promo cards have limited distribution and can be very expensive.

Proof card — A card produced by the card companies, prior to printing their sets, which is "proofed" for errors, and checked for card design, photography, colors, statistical accuracy and so on. Proof cards are not distributed and a few of the older proof cards on the hobby market can be quite expensive.

PPD — Postage Paid.

Rack pack — A three-sectioned card package with about 14-16 cards per section. There are usually 24 rack packs to a rack box, and six rack boxes to a rack case. Rack packs retail for a suggested price of $1 to $1.40 and are issued by Topps, Fleer, Donruss and Score.

Rare — Difficult to obtain and limited in number. See "Scarce."

Rated Rookie (RR) — A Donruss subset featuring young players the company thinks are the top rookie players from a particular year (1984-present).

Record Breaker card — A special Topps card found in a regular issue set which commemorates a record-breaking performance by a player from the previous season.

Regional set — A card set limited in distribution to one geographical area. Regional sets often depict players from one team.

Regular issue set — See "Major set."

Reprint cards — Cards reprinted to closely match original cards, made with the intention of allowing collectors to buy them as substitutes for cards they could never afford. Reprints are usually labled — but not always — "reprint."

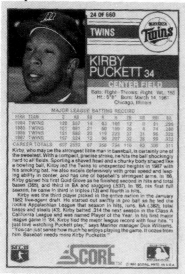

Reverse — The back of a card.

Rookie card (R or RC) — The first appearance of a player in one of the major sets (Topps, Fleer, etc.), excluding update and traded sets. It may or may not be issued during the player's actual rookie season.

ROY — Rookie of the Year.

SASE — Self-addressed stamped envelope.

Score (S or SC) — The brand name of baseball cards (1988-present). Major League Marketing is the manufacturer.

Score Traded (ScTr) — A 110-card post-season set issued by Score to include players traded during the season, as well as rookie players. Sold exclusively by hobby dealers in its own separate box.

Second-year card — The second card of a player issued in the major sets. Usually, a second-year card is the most expensive card of a player, next to the rookie card.

Sell price — The price for which a dealer is selling a card.

Series — A group of cards that is part of a set, and was issued at one time. The term usually applied to Topps sets from 1952-1973, when sets were issued in various "series." Cards of different series are valued at different prices since some series are scarcer than others.

Set — A complete run of cards, including one number of each card issued by a particular manufacturer in a particular year; for example, a 1985 Fleer "set."

General Information

Set case — Companies sell their factory sets in sealed cases containing eight to 16 sets per case, depending on the company. Issued by all major companies.

Skip-numbered — A set of cards not numbered in exact sequence. Some manufacturers have issued "skip-numbered" sets to trick collectors into buying more cards, looking for card numbers that didn't exist. Other sets became skip-numbered when one or more players were dropped from the set at the last minute and were not replaced with another.

Sleeve — A specially-designed plastic wrapper used to house and protect individual baseball cards.

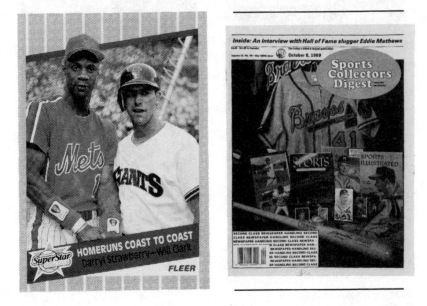

Special card — A card in a set that depicts something other than a single player, such as a checklist card, All-Star card, team card, team leaders card, etc.

Sportflics — A brand name of baseball cards (1986-present). These cards offer multi-images, such as a sequence of a batting motion with three separate pictures which can be seen by turning the card. Not popular among collectors. Major League Marketing is the manufacturer.

SCD — *Sports Collectors Digest.*

Standard size card — A card which measures 2½" by 3½" tall. In 1957, Topps baseball cards were produced in the 2½" by 3½" size, which set the standard for modern baseball cards.

Star card — A card featuring a star player, but not one of "superstar" caliber. The term "minor star" may also be used to differentiate between levels of skill and popularity. In terms of value, "star" cards fall between "commons" and "superstars."

Starter lot — A group of cards from the same set, usually more than 100, which serves as a starting point for a hobbyist to begin putting a set together.

Starter lots usually contain common players. Also known as a "starter set."

Starting Lineup — A line of plastic baseball, football and basketball action statues produced by Kenner (1988-present). Also, the name for a computer-based baseball game from Parker Brothers.

Sticker — An adhesive-backed baseball card. Stickers can be card-size or smaller. Topps, Fleer and Panini have issued major baseball sticker sets over the years. Stickers are not overly popular with older collectors, although younger collectors seem to enjoy them.

Subset — A set of cards with the same theme within a larger set. Examples: Donruss Diamond Kings are a "subset" of the Donruss set; or Topps All-Star cards are a subset of the Topps set.

Super card — A designation referring to the physical size of a card. Generally, any card postcard-size or larger is referred to as a "super."

Superstar card — A card picturing a true "superstar," a player of Hall of Fame caliber, such as Mike Schmidt.

Stock — Refers to the type of paper or cardboard used on a baseball card.

Swap meet — A term used to describe early baseball card shows in which a majority of cards were traded between hobbyists.

Team card — A card which depicts an entire team.

Team set — A set which includes all cards relating to a certain team from a particular year, by a particular manufacturer.

General Information

Team issued set — A set produced to be sold or given away by a baseball team. The cards may feature current or past players.

Test issue — A set of cards test-marketed on a small scale in limited geographic areas of the country. Topps test-marketed a variety of items from the 1950s-1980s.

Tobacco cards — Cards issued in the late 19th and early 20th centuries as premiums with cigarettes or other tobacco products.

Topps (T) — A baseball card company (1951-present). Topps currently produces baseball, non-sport, football and hockey cards.

Topps Tiffany (TTF) — A limited-edition set produced by Topps, featuring the year's regular complete set in a high-gloss finish (1984-present). Topps Traded sets are also done in this style.

Topps Traded (TT or TTR) — A 132-card post-season set which includes players traded to other teams during the year, as well as rookie players (1981 - present). They are sold exclusively through hobby dealers in their own separate box, although some of the 1989 sets were sold through major retail stores.

Traded set — An auxiliary set of cards issued toward the end of the season to reflect trades made after the printing of the regular set. Also called "Update" sets, they may also include rookies not included in the regular set.

Uncut sheet — A full sheet of baseball cards that has never been cut into individual cards.

Upper Deck (UD) — A baseball card company (1989-present). Upper Deck cards use a high quality stock, and retail at about twice the price of the other cards (Topps, etc.).

Upper Deck High Numbers (UDH) — A 100-card set featuring players traded during the season, as well as rookie players. This set was sold through hobby dealers and in Upper Deck foil packs, similar to the way cards before 1974 were released.

Variation — A variation is the result of a card company correcting a previous mistake on a card, resulting in two or more variations of the same card. Some variations have increased in value, if there were fewer produced.

Vending box — Vending boxes contain 500 cards per box. There are 24 vending boxes per vending case, for a total of 12,000 cards.

Want list — A collector's or dealer's list of items he is wishing to buy. Often, a collector will send a dealer a "want" list, and the dealer will try to locate the items on the list.

Wax pack — A wax pack contains 15-17 cards. Topps, Fleer and Donruss packs are wrapped in wax paper; Upper Deck is in a tin foil pack; Score and Sportflics are in a mylar package. There are usually 36 wax packs per wax box, and 20 wax boxes per wax case. Suggested retail prices range from 45 cents to $1.

General Information

Wrong backs — A card with the wrong back (the player on the front does not match the biography/statistics on the back). Most collectors think these cards are damaged and are worth less than a correctly-printed card, although some collectors will pay premiums on superstars or rookies.

Further Reading

Books

Baker, Mark Allen. *Baseball Autograph Handbook,* Second Edition. Krause Publications, Iola, Wisconsin, 1991.

Baker, Mark Allen. *Team Baseballs, A Comprehensive Guide to Autographed Team Baseballs.* Krause Publications, Iola, Wisconsin, 1992.

Clark, Steve. *The Complete Book of Baseball Cards.* Grosset & Dunlap, New York, 1976.

Kurowski, Jeff. *Baseball Card Price Guide,* 6th edition. Krause Publications, Iola, Wisconsin, 1992.

Kurowski, Jeff. *Standard Catalog of Baseball Cards,* Third Edition. Krause Publications, Iola, Wisconsin, 1992.

Lemke, Bob. *Sportscard Counterfeit Detector.* Krause Publications, Iola, Wisconsin, 1992.

Football, Basketball and Hockey Price Guide. by the editors of Sports Collectors Digest, Krause Publications, Iola, Wisconsin, 1991.

Periodicals

Published by Krause Publications, 700 E. State St., Iola, Wis. 54990. For advertising or subscription information, write to the above address.

Baseball Cards magazine (monthly, 12 issues a year)

Card News (biweekly, 26 issues a year); formerly Baseball Card News.

Fantasy Baseball (quarterly, four issues a year)

Sports Card Price Guide Monthly (monthly, 12 issues a year); formerly Baseball Cards Price Guide Monthly.

Sports Collectors Digest (weekly, 52 issues a year)

All prices quoted in this book are current through March of 1992.

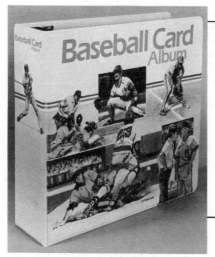

Card Grading and Taking Care of Your Cards

Chapter Two

What are the grading standards for baseball cards?

The following list and illustrations should give you a better idea of the different card grades or conditions:

Mint (Mt.): A perfect card. Well-centered, with equal borders. Four sharp, square corners. No creases, edge dents, surface scratches, paper flaws, loss of luster, yellowing or fading, regardless of age. No imperfectly printed card (out of register, badly cut or ink-flawed) or card stained by contact with gum, wax or other substances can truly be considered Mint, even if it's new out of the pack.

Mint

Cards from 1948-1980 in Mint condition are valued from 25-75 percent higher than cards in Near Mint condition.

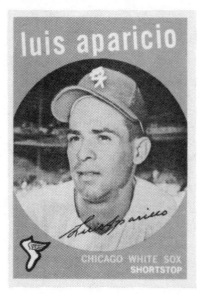

Near Mint (Nr. Mt.): A nearly perfect card. At first glance, a Near Mint card appears perfect; under closer examination, however, a minor flaw will be discovered. On well-centered cards, three of the four corners must be perfectly sharp. A slightly off-center card would also fit this grade.

Near Mint

When values for cards issued between 1948-80 are quoted in Krause Publications' price quides, they are the guide price for a card or set in Near Mint condition. This is the most popular grade for investment quality cards, and the highest feasible condition in which cards or sets can be built. Percentages of the Near Mint value are used when calculating values for all other grades.

Excellent (Ex.): Corners are more sharp than rounded. Card borders may be off center. No creases. No gum, wax or product stains, front or back. Surfaces may show some loss of luster.

Excellent

Cards from 1981-present in Excellent condition are valued from 20-40 percent of cards in Mint condition. There is no market for cards issued from 1981-present in less than Excellent condition.

Very Good (VG): Shows obvious handling. Corners are rounded and/or perhaps show minor creases. Other minor creases may be visible. Surfaces may exhibit loss of luster, but all printing is intact. May show gum, wax or other packaging stains. No major creases, tape marks or extraneous markings or writing. Exhibits honest wear.

JOE MORGAN   2nd base

Very Good

Cards from 1948-1980 in Very Good condition are valued at 30 percent of cards in Near Mint condition.

Good (G): A well-worn card with no intentional damage or abuse. May have major or multiple creases. Corners are rounded well beyond the border.

Good

Cards from 1948-1980 in Good condition are valued at 15 percent of cards in Near Mint condition.

FRANK ROBINSON
Outfield-First Base   Cincinnati
                          Reds

Fair (F): Shows excessive wear, along with damage or abuse, such as thumbtack holes in or near margins, evidence of having been taped or pasted, perhaps small tears around the edges, or creases so heavy as to break the cardboard. Backs may show minor added writing or be missing small bits of paper. Still, a basically complete card.

Fair

Cards from 1948-1980 in Fair condition are valued at 7 percent of cards in Near Mint condition.

Poor (P): A card that has been tortured to death. Corners or other areas may be torn off. Cards may have been trimmed, show holes from a paper punch or have been used for BB-gun practice. Fronts may have extraneous pen or

Poor

Generally, there is no market value for cards which are in Poor condition.

pencil writing or other defacement. Major portions of front and back design may be missing. Not a pretty sight.

In addition to these grades, collectors will often encounter intermediate grades, such as VG-EX. (Very Good to Excellent), Ex.-Mt. (Excellent to Mint) or Nr. Mt.-Mt. (Near Mint to Mint). Intermediate grades are used to indicate that a card has all the characteristics of the lower grade, with enough of those of the higher grade to merit mention. Such cards are usually priced at a point midway between the two grades.

Common Grading
Terms & Definitions

Chipping — Refers to card borders which are worn away, usually on cards with dark-colored borders such as 1971 Topps cards.

Crease — A wrinkle in a card caused in the manufacturing process or by careless handling. A crease greatly reduces the value of the card.

Ding — A dent or other slight damage to the borders or corners of cards.

Gum stain — The stain on a card caused by the gum inside the pack. One way to remove these stains on the front of a card with little risk of damage is to lightly rub a nylon stocking over the stain. A stained card is worth less than an unstained card.

Layering — The separation of the layers of paper that make up the cardboard stock. Layering is a sign of wear that is first noticeable at the corners of the card.

Luster — The amount of glossiness on the card front. Cards which show a lack of luster are decreased slightly in value.

Miscut — A card that has been cut incorrectly from a press sheet during the manufacturing process and is thus decreased in value.

Notching — Indentations along the edge of a card, sometimes caused by a rubber band. Notching decreases a card's value. Also known as "edge dent."

Off-center (o/c) — A card with uneven borders. Cards are often described as "slightly off-center" (Sl.o/c), or by a percentage of the amount the card is off-center, such as "60/40" or "70/30". The more off-center a card, the lower its value.

Out-of-register — A printing error in which the various colors are not correctly superimposed upon one another, thereby decreasing the value of the card.

Restored card — A card which has its imperfections fixed long after the card was issued. A card restorer can fix corners and creases, and restore gloss to the stock of a card. Restored cards should be labeled clearly by the seller, and should be priced much less than unrestored cards in the same condition.

Scuff — A rub or abrasion on a card which removes a portion of its gloss, lessening the value of a card.

Trimmed card — A card that has been cut down from its original size, greatly reducing its value. In order to tell if a card has been trimmed, either measure it, or compare it to a card from the same set which is known not to have been trimmed.

Wax stain — A stain caused by the wax wrappers baseball cards are sold in. A wax stain usually affects the bottom card of a wax pack. For an explanation of how to remove wax stains, see "Gum stain."

Why are there grading standards?

These standards are necessary because buyers and sellers need a frame of reference to reach an informed agreement on a card's value, especially when buying and selling by mail.

What effect does a card's grade have on its value?

Card collectors may be the most finicky of all collectors when it comes to the condition of their items. Most collectors want only top condition cards. Thus, grade is vitally important to the value of a card. Without exception, the better the condition of the card, the greater its value. Take for instance the 1973 Topps Mike Schmidt card. As of 1992, this Schmidt card in Near Mint condition was valued at $450, while the card in Excellent condition was valued at $225. Lower grade cards sell for even less.

Is there a sure way not to get taken when selling cards? Suppose I think a card is Near Mint and a buyer says it is only Excellent? Are they any recognized services that grade cards?

The only sure way to avoid getting taken when selling, or buying, a card is to learn how to grade properly, and then stand by your opinion. It is natural that a seller wants to get as much for your card as possible, and the buyer wants to pay as little as possible. Ultimately, the buyer makes the final decision; he can either buy the card at your price and grade, or just say no. There are no widely-advertised card grading services — yet. But we expect that situation to change in the coming years.

What is the highest you would grade an otherwise Near Mint card which has pencil marks on the back?

With pencil marks, no higher than Very Good.

Years ago I purchased a 1952 Gil Hodges card and paid a good buck for it. The card has a scrape on the left front. A collector (questionable) told me the card is worthless. What do you think? If it's not worthless, do you think it's at least worth 50 percent of the book price?

Because of the rounding at all four corners, even without the scrape the card would grade Excellent. For low number 1952 Topps cards, Excellent cards are worth only about 45 to 60 percent of Near Mint value to begin with. When you consider this scrape is actually a small piece of the card's picture torn away, it lowers the grade to Fair. If a Near Mint '52 Hodges is currently worth $150, a Fair card has a value of around $15. However, since "books" don't buy and sell cards, you are free to value it as you please — as is any prospective buyer.

What effect does centering have on the value of a card? Can a card that comes right from the pack, but has barely any border on one side, be considered Mint?

It can be considered new, but not Mint. If you doubt that, try selling a badly off-center card to a dealer for his advertised Mint buying price. If you're buying cards for possible future appreciation, steer well clear of off-center cards.

I took my Eric Davis rookie card to a dealer and asked him to appraise it. He said it was basically worthless because it was too far off center. My brother bought this for me as a gift and paid top dollar for it.

Your brother did not shop wisely. (Having seen the card), not only is it off center, it is also cross-cut. (Cross-cut means the borders are thicker at one end of the card than the other.) Your card cannot even be graded as high as Near Mint.

What would you grade a card that is in Mint condition, except that it is not well-centered? The border on the left is about twice the size of the border on the right.

If a border is showing on the right side, you have a Near Mint card.

A friend of mine says off-centered cards can be considered Mint. He says perfectly-centered cards are considered "Gem Mint," and bring higher-than-book value. Is this true or is my friend trying to trade me all his off-centered cards?

Your friend is out of date. First, there is no such recognized card condition as "Gem Mint." Though the term is used frequently in the hobby, it is a term that does not officially exist. Second, the most widely-used published card grading standards require a card to be well-centered to be considered Mint.

If a card is off-center, is it considered an error? Can it be Mint?

A card that is noticeably off-center at first glance cannot be considered Mint. It is considered a printing error only if it is so far off-center that part of another card shows on it. Such cards have little or no premium value.

My friend says cards that are cut wrong — half of one player, half of another — are worthless. Is he right?

Yes. Most collectors consider miscut cards to be damaged and, therefore, worth far less money.

If the face of a card is touched, is it still in Mint condition?

As long as the touch doesn't damage the card in any way. Mint means perfect when examined closely, not that the card has never been touched by human hands.

I have a 1978 Paul Molitor/Alan Trammell rookie card. The card is in Mint condition, except that some of the "Rookie Shortstops" printing is smeared onto the white border. Does this effect the condition/price of the card?

Definitely. A card cannot be Mint if it exhibits a printing flaw of this nature. Unfortunately, a huge percentage of the Molitor/Trammell rookie cards have the smeared printing; finding a truly Mint card can be a real challenge. The type of flaw downgrades a card to no better than Near Mint grade/price.

I have a card with four very sharp corners, and there is almost no luster gone. There is a small stain on the left border of the card. What grade would this card fit?

Unless the "stain" is a printing or packaging flaw, a card with a noticeable added substance can technically grade no better than Good, although if it is otherwise visually appealing, it may sell for more than the average Good card.

If a Mint card has a wax or gum stain on the back, will it affect the value of the card?

If your card has a gum or wax stain, then it's not a Mint card. Depending on how heavy the stain, the card might be graded as low as Very Good. Dealers who advertise an expensive card of this nature may explain the card's flaw as "Mint corners, gum stain on back."

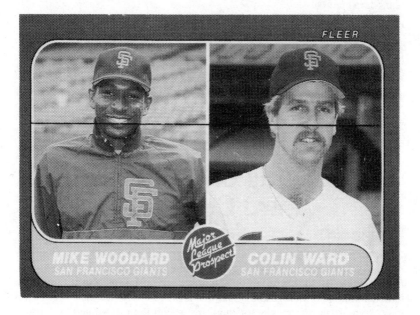

I have a couple of 1986 Fleer "Major League Prospects" cards that have a thin blue line — must be an error in the printing — across the length of the card. How much, if any, does this decrease the value of the card?

It depends on whether the rookies pictured get to be superstars or otherwise in high demand. If the cards stay a common, a minor printing flaw will not generally be of concern to 90 percent of the collectors. If, however, the card ever starts to sell for big money, most buyers will demand perfection, and you'll likely have to take 25 to 50 percent off the Mint price to make a sale.

On my 1987 Topps Eric Davis and Jose Canseco cards there are little green dots — three next to Canseco's head and three on the right side of Davis' body. Can these cards be considered Mint?

All the 1987 Topps Davis and Canseco cards we've seen contain the small green dots. The dots are very small and only noticeable by looking closely. Since the dots were on the original negative and are not a printing-press malfunction, they can be considered Mint.

I have 1987 and 1988 Fleer baseball card sets. On the back of almost all the cards, the cards are chipped at the top and bottom. Does this chipping do anything to the price of the cards?

Not necessarily. If these are particularly rare or desirable cards, and the person you are selling them to is holding out for ultimate condition, then he may not be willing to pay absolute top dollar for them. But I doubt very seriously whether this light chipping will make much of a difference to the average buyer of modern material.

A friend of mine gave me a 1977 Dale Murphy rookie. The card is in good condition, except there is a hole that has been punched with a hole puncher in the corner. Does this destroy the value of the card?

Yes. A card with a hole punched in it can be considered no higher than Poor in condition. Few collectors are interested in cards which grade that low.

Taking Care of Your Card Collection

We cannot understate the importance of properly protecting and storing your baseball cards. Improper storage can ruin and devalue your cards. Years ago, rubber bands and shoe boxes were all that was available to hobbyists. Today, we have a multitude of storage and display items that are very reasonably priced. As long as you spent the money for the cards, spend the extra dollars to protect them right.

Could you explain the different types of card sleeves, sheets and boxes?

As far as sleeves (or holders) for individual cards, there are basically three types. The first is a soft, floppy plastic sleeve, generally used for less-expensive cards; these sleeves sell for around one to two cents each. The second is a semi-rigid or plastic sleeve which better protects cards than the soft sleeves, and is used for more expensive cards; they cost from 10-25 cents each. The third is a

hard plastic holder which comes in two pieces and either snaps or is screwed together to hold the card; these holders are used for the most expensive cards and cost from $2-$4 each.

There are several different kinds of plastic sheets available, some of which you load the cards from the top of the pockets, some from the sides. The most common is the nine-pocket sheet which fits most cards from 1957-present. Other sheets are available to fit cards of different measurements. These sheets retail for around 10-15 cents each. These sheets are produced to fit into three-ring baseball card albums (binders), with many sheets fitting in each album. The albums range in price from $4-$6, depending on the size (2" or 3" spine) and quality. Also available are display sheets with up to 30 pockets that can be hung on the wall. These are great for displaying team sets.

There are many different types of baseball card boxes. Some cardboard boxes hold as few 100 cards, while others hold 5,000. The 800-count and 660-count boxes are the most common; they hold Topps and Upper Deck sets (800-count), and most Fleer, Donruss and Score sets (660-count). The larger boxes are given names such as the "shoe box" (1,600 cards), the "monster box" (3,200 cards), and the "super monster box" (5,000 cards). Prices range, depending on the number of cards they can hold, from 30 cents to $2. There are also smaller plastic "snap" boxes that hold from 1-100 cards; they are priced from 25-50 cents each. There are many, many other types of card display supplies, including those for bats and autographed balls. Look over the selection of supplies at your local card shop or the next show you attend to see which kinds appeal to you.

I recently bought a package of card sleeves advertised as being made of "polypropylene." I notice that most sleeves are made of polyethylene. Is one type a better quality than the other?

The polypropylene sleeve is a bit less opaque (more clear) than the polyethylene, but the seams at the side tear much more easily. You have to choose whether clarity or strength is more important to you.

What is PVC? How does it harm the cards? What will safely store my cards for years?

PVC is polyvinylchloride, the common name for a type of flexible plastic often used to make sheets for holding cards. It can harm cards because over the years some of the chemicals of which it is formulated are prone to migrating out of the plastic onto whatever is held inside. This was a much bigger problem 10 years ago when most plastic pages were very cheaply made. Today, better materials are used to produce sheets that are perfectly adequate for most collectors' storage needs. The best protection for long-term storage, if you won't be handling the cards, is the use of acid-free cardboard boxes.

I am currently keeping my cards in a magnetic photo album. Will this damage them?

We would be concerned with the tacky material on the pages that makes them magnetic. This gluey substance could theoretically stain the back of your cards.

I just bought some airtight plastic holders for some of my more expensive baseball cards. Will it hurt the cards because they are airtight?

For practical purposes, no. Even if the holders were actually airtight, they would not harm your cards for decades. In theory, if cheap paper (the kind on which most baseball cards are printed) is kept in airtight conditions, not allowing the paper to "breathe," the release of the natural humidity in the paper, plus the many acids and chemicals it contains, will harm the card. This process, however, may take a lifetime. Since most cards are popped in and out of their holders every couple of months or years, I wouldn't worry about it; such holders will protect your cards from lots of worse things that could happen to them.

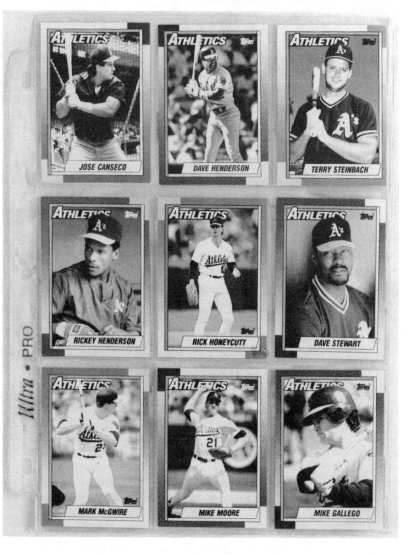

A friend of mine says that putting two baseball cards back-to-back in a pocket of a plastic sheet will ruin the backs of those cards. Is this true?

You may ding a corner on a card if you don't use care in placing the cards in the pocket. Otherwise, no damage should occur.

I have some cards I have been having difficulty locating plastic sheets for. The cards measure 3¼" by 5½." Could you help?

Yes and no. First, resign yourself to the fact that you will not find plastic sheets that will exactly fit your cards. Your cards have such seldom-seen dimensions that no sheetmaker is going to keep an inventory of sheets that exactly match these specifications. However, many companies make and advertise sheets to fit 4" by 6" postcards, 5" by 7" photos and 3½" by 5½" photos. These sheets should do the trick for you.

Is it better to buy the snap-together plastic card holders that have a recessed area for the card? In other words, is the pressure of the non-recessed holders bad for the cards?

The utility and safety of any card-holding supplies, including sheets or holders, must be assessed on a piece-by-piece basis as even those that look similar can have important differences. Generally, those holders which have recessed space for the cards hold the danger that the card might be damaged while getting it properly aligned into the hole and snapped shut. The danger with holders consisting of two flat pieces of plastic screwed together is that the face of the card might be scratched when the screws are tightened. With proper handling, either is safe for your cards.

I overheard two card dealers talking about framing the Topps Stadium Club cards in acrylic frames and saying this could damage the cards because of their glossy finish. Is there any truth to that?

Could be. There have been proven cases of glossy-finish cards being damaged by storage in certain types of plastic sheets, notably those formulated of polyvinyl chloride. Since this type of damage can take a long time to develop, depending on heat, humidity and pressure of the storage system, it may be a while before we can learn what's safe and what isn't for today's new generation of glossy cards.

At what type of temperature should I store my cards?

The best place is a cool room with little humidity and no direct sunlight. Also, try to store your cards off the floor to guard against a broken water pipe or other such water hazards.

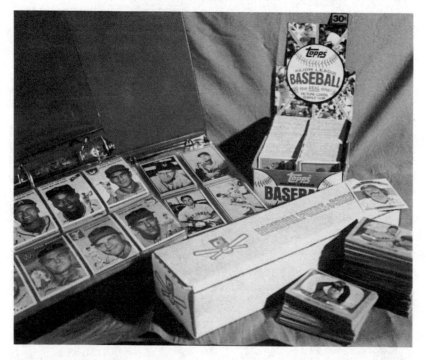

How can I prevent my cards from warping? I have them in boxes and in pages, but some still warp. Also, does the warp decrease the value of a card?

The warping is a natural process as the cardboard ages and takes on humidity. You can prevent it only by packing them so tightly in a box that they can't bend, or by placing your pages flat and keeping some weight on them.

Surprisingly, a natural curve in a card is not viewed by most collectors and dealers as a defect, as long is does not affect the card by causing creasing.

If you put a card with wrinkles (creases) in a ziplock bag and ironed over it, would it take out some of the wrinkles?

No. It would just melt the plastic bag all over your card. While it is true that some restoration artists can remove creases from cards, it does not change the grade or true value.

Is protecting a card in plastic using a laminating machine OK, or will the card's value diminish?

From a value standpoint, laminating a card is a no-no. If you laminate a card, you have altered it from its original state. The plastic coating cannot be removed without damaging the card. If you can get 10 percent of the price guide value of a laminated card, consider yourself lucky.

If Topps cards are left unopened in their packs, will the gum harm the cards?

Yes. Depending on the storage conditions, the gum starts to dissolve in a couple of years, and will eventually weld itself onto the card it's resting on. That's not so bad if the card is Don Aase, but it can be tragic if it's Don Mattingly.

I have an uncut sheet of 1984 Topps/Nestles cards with Don Mattingly, Darryl Strawberry, etc. I telephoned a local framing store to get a price for framing, but I found it would be very expensive. How can I inexpensively display it without damaging it?

There is a substance on the market called Blu-Tack which sells for about a dollar. It will hang your cards without damaging them if it is rolled off instead of peeled off when you want to take down the sheet. The adhesive is reusable and a pack will hold quite a few sheets if used properly. You can find Blu-Tack in stores near the glues, tapes and other adhesives.

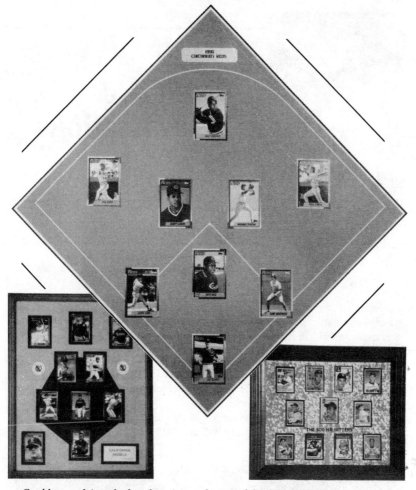

Could you advise whether there is any danger of displaying baseball cards in picture frames on the wall? They are kept out of direct sunlight but we are concerned that there could be fading caused by indirect sunlight or artificial light.

Baseball cards, like most printed items, will eventually fade if exposed to ultraviolet light, either from the sun or from artificial light. There are UV filters available for some lights, and some types of glass and plastic are available that will filter out UV. Left unprotected, your cards will show noticeable fading in just a couple of years.

How do I get ahold of a computer disk to keep inventory of my baseball cards? My computer is an Apple II GS.

There are several companies offering computer inventories. Watch the ads in *Baseball Cards* magazine and *Sports Collectors Digest,* including the classified ads pages.

Card Identifications

Chapter Three

Pre-1929 Cards

I recently found a Near Mint condition card (#68) of Honus Wagner in my grandmother's attic. It has Cracker Jack written on the back and appears to be from a set issued in 1915 or 1916. Can you tell me anything about this card? Does it have any value?

It sure does. Cracker Jack cards were made in 1914 and 1915 and were given away inside packages of the confection. They're uniformly valuable cards in high grades, as well as a collector favorite.

While the most valuable of the set is Ty Cobb, a top-grade Wagner will bring about $2,800 in the 1914 set, and $2,000 in the 1915 set. Sets can be distinguished

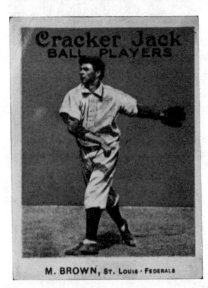

by the backs; card backs from the 1914 set say the set is complete at 144 cards, while backs from the 1915 set say the set is complete at 176. A complete set and album was available from the company.

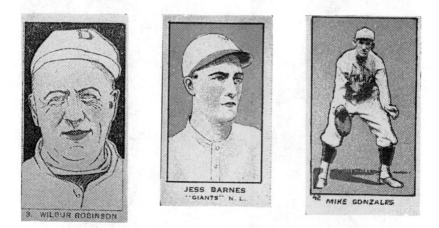

I have some W-series cards I can't identify. They're probably from 1920-1923, but they don't fit any descriptions in the guides I've looked at. They come in pairs of two. The pairs I have are Ruth-Cobb, Barnes-Stengel, Johnson-Sisler, Pipp-Speaker, and Bancroft-F. Baker. What can you tell me about them?

The cards are from a 10-card set known by collectors as the W-551 strip-card set. It's not a common set, but also not that attractive, so the two factors cancel each other out. A complete set in Near Mint condition sells for $1,250. The cards are checklisted and valued in the *Standard Catalog of Baseball Cards.* (See examples of strip cards above.)

I purchased three cards I can't find in any books. On the back of the cards is a list of 30 names from the 1910 era, such as Cy Young and Ty Cobb, leading me to believe they are from a set of 30 cards. Could I have a find on my hands?

Sorry, no big find. You must have been looking in the wrong books. Your cards can be found in the *Standard Catalog of Baseball Cards.* They are from the 30-card set issued in 1911, known by its *American Card Catalog* number of E-94. Commons are valued at $185 in top grade, to $4,500 for the Cobb.

Recently my son received a small collection of old baseball cards as a gift. I have identified them from the front of the cards; they are Zeenut cards. All are black-and-white photo cards. They measure 1¼" by 2¾". Where can I find out more on them?

One of the largest (nearly 4,000 different known) and longest-running (1911-

Card Identifications

1938) baseball card issues of all time, the Zeenut cards were produced by a San Francisco area candy company. They feature only players of the Pacific Coast League. Originally issued with coupons on the bottom, they are very seldom found that way today. Because they are not widely collected — nobody owns a "complete" collection — they have not developed much value. Common player cards in Very Good condition sell for $3-$5 apiece.

A friend of mine recently found three baseball cards while moving. They are 1913 Fatima team pictures of the Philadelphia Athletics, Boston Braves and Pittsburgh Nationals. Can you give me more information on these?

Collectors call this issue T-200. It consists of team cards of all 16 major league teams in 1913. Values range from $250-$700 in Near Mint condition for the 2⅜" by 4⅞" version of the cards. Much larger versions (13" by 21") were also issued. They are worth from 12-15 times the value of the smaller cards.

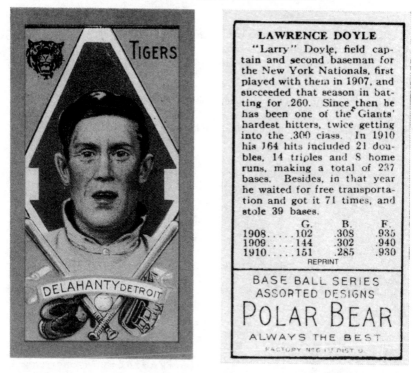

I recently purchased a card I believe was made in 1911, since the last year in statistics on the card back is 1910. The player is Jim Delehanty of the Detroit Tigers. An advertisement for Polar Bear cigarettes appears on the back. Can you help me identify this card?

Your card is one of 217 from the 1911 T-205 Gold Border set, which was issued in packs of several different cigarette brands. The cards measure 1½" by 2⅞". Delehanty is a common player in the set, and sells for $100 in Near Mint condition. The T-205 is a very popular set.

1930-1949 Cards

*Every price guide I've ever seen states there was no card #126 issued in the 1939 Play Ball set. However, in the book **Classic Baseball Cards** there is a card pictured and numbered 126. It is a Chicago White Sox player — I think it's Monty Stratton. I hope you can solve the mystery because it's very strange.*

Card Identifications

We can't say for sure, but we think the producers of the book took some liberties and created a card #126 so there wouldn't be a gap in their book. Nobody has ever reported a legitimate 1939 Play Ball card of Monty Stratton.

I have an arcade card my father gave me some years ago. On the card are Mickey Cochrane, Charlie Gehringer, Goose Goslin and Linwood Rowe. The card measures 3⅜" by 5⅜". Can you tell me the name of the manufacturer and the date it was printed?

Your card was produced in 1937 and sold in penny arcade machines. The card was issued by the Exhibit Supply Co. of Chicago. Exhibit Supply issued cards from the 1920s through the mid-1960s. Your card is valued at $30 in Excellent condition.

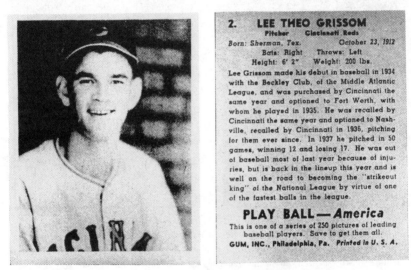

I was given two baseball cards for my birthday. The pictures are black-and-white with no team logo or player name on the front. The most recent year mentioned on the back is 1938. The back says, "Play Ball — America." Can you give me information on these cards?

Your cards are from the popular 1939 Play Ball set, the first of three annual sets produced by Gum Inc. (a Bowman predecessor). The 1939 set featured most of the stars of the day, and was the first major set since the 1934 Goudey. Common players in Very Good condition can be found for about $6 apiece. The Joe DiMaggio and Ted Williams "rookie" cards in this set can bring more than $1,500 each in top grade.

I decided to unearth some old baseball cards of mine to see if they have any value.

Among them are a Joe DiMaggio, Goudey #274, and Joe Marty, #216. I haven't been able to find them in any guides. What can you tell me about them?

They sure do have value. The Goudey card is from 1938. This set, Goudey's last real collectible issue, is commonly known as the "Heads Up" set because of the photo head on a cartoon body. The DiMaggio in top condition is valued at $3,500. The other card is from the 1940 Play Ball set which contained 240 cards. Your card, in top shape, is valued at $80.

I have a glossy photo of Earl Averill that measures 6" by 8". There is no other

identification on it. Any idea what it is and when it was printed?

Your photo is from the 1936 set known to collectors as R311. There were 28 individual player and team photos. They were issued as a premium, probably by one of the gum companies of the day. Values of the cards in Near Mint condition range from $15-$150.

I have a "Baseball's Great Hall Of Fame" card of Honus Wagner. What can you tell me about it?

Your card is one of a 32-card set produced by the Exhibit Supply Co. of Chicago in 1948. A Near Mint card is valued at $3, with the whole set at $500. Twenty-four of the cards, including the Wagner card, were reissued in 1974. These reprints can be identified by the extremely white stock they were printed on.

My uncle asked me to find out the value and history of a Ty Cobb card. On the back, it says card #13. The card is brown and I think it came out of a bubble gum pack.

Your card is from the 1948 252-card "Magic Photos" set. It's one of the first Topps sets, and featured baseball and football players, boxers, wrestlers, track-and-field stars, actors, dogs, aviation pioneers, famous landmarks and general sports pictures. The cards were "developed" by moistening them and exposing them to sunlight. Since some of the cards have better photographic sensitivity than others, not all cards develop well. Poorly developed cards are worth about one-third to one-half the value of properly developed cards. Your Cobb card is worth about $100 in top condition.

A fellow collector was showing me a set of old cards he just picked up. They are

55

supposed to be cards from 1947 issued by the Bond Bread Co. The problem is, I looked up the cards and the only Bond Bread cards I could find had Jackie Robinson on the entire set and stats on the back. My friend's cards are blank on the back. Some are cut wrong and they are just too perfect to be 42-year-old cards. Are these cards real? I hope so. He paid an arm and a leg for them.

The cards are real. They are Homogenized Bond Bread cards of 1947. A large hoard of 24 of the 48 cards issued in that set in 1947 was found some years ago. A major promotion was recently run in the national media offering the cards at a high, though fair, price. The entire set, in Near Mint condition, is valued at $600.

1950-1959 Cards

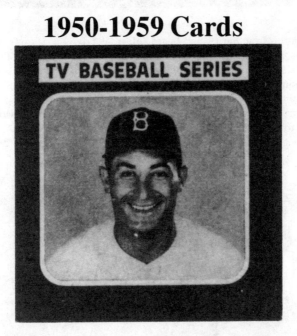

I found two "television" cards in my grandmother's attic — Alvin Dark and Dick Sisler. I didn't know Drake's put out cards in 1950. What do you know about these cards? I haven't seen them at card shows — perhaps they aren't worth anything.

Au contraire. In top grades, even commons such as Dark and Sisler are worth up to $50 each, while the Hall of Famers such as Spahn and Berra can bring more than $225 each. In all, there are 36 cards in the set. You don't see them at shows because they are really quite scarce.

I have some cards that came in envelopes with the team name in red. The cards have no picture, but include players' names, personal information and numbers like "11-5" and "51-8." Some players I have heard of, some are older players. What are they? When were they produced? Are they scarce? Are they worth keeping?

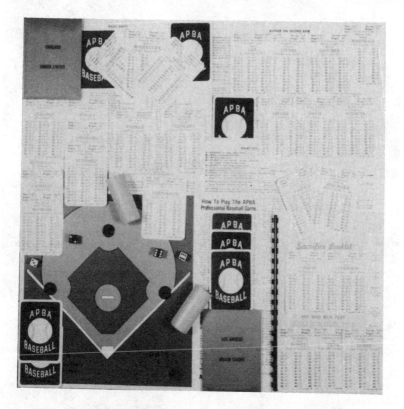

These are called "Ap-bah" cards by collectors, from the game with which they have been issued since 1951. APBA is a dice baseball game in which players' on-field performances are supposedly translated to the odds of rolling a particular combination on a pair of dice.

Surprisingly, some people collect these pictureless cards. The 1950 set, produced in 1951, would bring as much as $5,000 today. (It has since been reprinted.) Each new year's cards to update the game cost $15-$20, and there is now a computerized version of the game.

My aunt recently gave me a collection of cards. Some of the 1952 Topps cards have symbols such as "1/Bunt" in the corners. What do they mean?

Those are 1951 Topps cards, not 1952. The round-cornered 1951 Topps cards measure 2" by 2⅝" and were issued with either a "blue back" or "red back," with the blue backs being more scarce. The "Series of 52" printed on the cards indi-

cated the number of cards in the set. The symbols in the corners were used for playing a game of baseball with the cards.

Could you please tell me all available information about Red Man chewing tobacco baseball cards?

It would take a feature-length article to do that. Here's a brief summary: Red Mans were issued from 1952-1955 in sets of 50 or 52 cards a year, evenly divided between American and National League stars. Value depends not only on the year of issue, player and condition, but whether the ¼" mail-in tab at the bottom of the card is still there. Commons without tabs can be had in Near Mint condition for around $8 apiece, while top-grade Hall of Famers with tabs bring $50-$100. Cards with tabs are worth twice as much as cards without them.

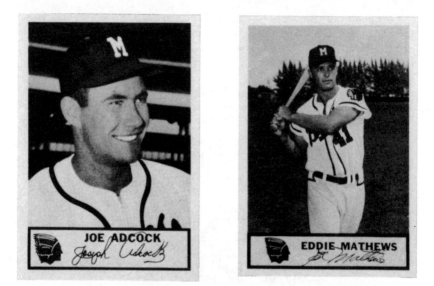

My dad has some 1953 Johnston Cookie Co. cards of Billy Bruton, Jim Wilson, Sid Gordon and Joe Adcock. What can you tell me about them?

They're nice cards. Milwaukee's Johnston Cookie Co. (you can see the factory from Milwaukee County Stadium) inserted Milwaukee Braves baseball cards into cookie boxes from 1953-1955. The 1953 set is the easiest to find, and is comprised of 25 well-done colorizations of black-and-white photos. A complete set is worth $325 in Near Mint condition. The cards you mentioned are worth $8-$12 each.

The card companies begin planning their sets a year or more in advance. Bowman's last issue came in 1955, and then it was bought out by Topps. Were any designs created by Bowman for anticipated sets? Are there any 1956 Bowman proofs circulating in the hobby?

There are reportedly seven different card designs considered by Bowman for 1956. It was narrowed down to three, and proof cards for each design do exist.

One style is similar to cards in the 1953 Bowman Color set, except that the player's name, position and team appear on the card front. The second proof card features a player's photo as seen through a large knothole in a fence. The third proof card is designed in a horizontal format. Two photos, one portrait and the other an action shot, share the card equally. The three proof cards are blank-backed.

Card Identifications

I found some baseball cards in a box entitled "Who's Who in Major League Baseball Presents Pictures and Records of the Immortals of the Baseball Hall of Fame." The backs of the cards indicate they were issued by B.E. Callahan in either 1950 or 1952. Can you identify these cards?

Your cards were produced by the B.E. Callahan Corp., for sale by the Baseball Hall of Fame in Cooperstown. The cards feature black-and-white drawings and measure 1¾" by 2½" in size. The first sets were produced in 1950 with new cards added each year through 1956 as more players were inducted into the HOF.

Since certain cards were produced in all seven years, only those which feature 1955 and 1956 inductees are considered scarce. Most cards sell for $1 apiece; however, cards of Babe Ruth and Ty Cobb are valued at $40 each.

1952 — Back To The Marines

Ted's Idol — Babe Ruth

I have a Ted Williams card that was made by Fleer. What can you tell me about it?

In 1959, Fleer produced an 80-card set telling the life story of Ted Williams. The cards are the standard 2½" by 3½". Card #68 was withdrawn shortly after production of the set and is very scarce. The majority of the cards sell for $3 each in Near Mint condition, with the set valued at $700. A complete checklist can be found in the 6th edition of the *Sports Collectors Digest Baseball Card Price Guide*.

I bought 1958 Topps Stan Musial and Eddie Mathews Sport Magazine All-Star cards. What can you tell me about them?

The *Sport* All-Stars are a small subset of the regular 1958 Topps set. They're the equivalent of current Topps All-Star cards. Back then, putting *Sport* magazine's name on the card gave the whole thing an air of authenticity; now it's not really necessary. The Musial is valued at $7.50, and the Mathews at $3.50, in Very Good condition.

I bought a Luke Easter card that I know very little about. It has a "Bond Bread" advertisement on the back. Can you shed any information on it?

The Coleman card is one of nine unnumbered black-and-white baseball cards issued by Bond Bread in 1958. The cards, which featured members of the minor league Buffalo Bisons, were inserted into packages of Bond Bread products.

1960-1969 Cards

I discovered several Reds and Indians sets from, I believe, 1964. I have been unable to find them in any price guide and would appreciate any information you could give me on them.

Your sets are from Kahn's Weiners, part of a series issued regionally between 1955 and 1969. They are quite scarce and popular with collectors. Check the sixth edition of the *SCD Baseball Card Price Guide* annual for more data.

I own some cards of old-time players. The cards are 2½" by 3½" and have perforated edges. The backs have career stats, a brief biography and the year the player was elected into the Hall of Fame. Can you identify these cards?

Your cards are part of the 1961 Golden Press set which contains 33 Hall of Famers. The cards were part of a booklet with perforations so the cards could be removed easily. A complete set of single cards is valued at $65 in Near Mint condition. A full book, with the cards intact, would command a 50 percent premium.

Will you help me identify the Baltimore Orioles manager card (#131) of Paul Richards?

Your card is one of 17 manager cards included in the 1961 Topps set. Card numbers for the manager cards are 131-139 and 219-226.

I have an MVP card of Al Rosen that I have been unable to identify. On the front it says "Most Valuable Player — 1953 American League," with Rosen's picture and name.

The card is from a 16-card sequence (cards #471-486) in the regular 1961 Topps set honoring MVPs from 1950-1960.

I have an Exhibit card of Lou Gehrig I can't find in any price guide or publication. Could you give me the background on this card? I think I got it for a penny in the early 1960s.

You have part of the 24-card set issued in vending machines at Wrigley Field in Chicago in 1961. The players are Hall of Famers. Values for Near Mint cards range from $4 for commons to $50 for Babe Ruth, according to the *Standard Catalog of Baseball Cards*.

I bought a Lou Gehrig card from a shop and have since forgotten the year and what it's worth. It has a drawn picture of Gehrig holding his bat in his left hand. His name is printed in white on a blue pennant. On the back is printed "Baseball Greats." Few people I have talked to have seen it. It is card #31.

Your card is from the 1961-1962 Fleer set of 154 former players. The cards are rather scarce, but they are not very valuable. In typical condition, the Gehrig is a $3-$6 card.

Card Identifications

I recently bought a Babe Ruth card. On the front, under his name, it says "Baseball Hero." What kind of card is it? What year is it? Was $30 too much?

You've been had. This Ruth card is from a 44-card Topps non-sport set issued in 1967 called "Who am I?" The cards were issued with black "disguises" and clues on the front which could be rubbed off to reveal the person beneath. The only players in the set were Babe Ruth, Willie Mays, Mickey Mantle and Sandy Koufax. The value on them is $3-$5, tops.

I have an old five-cent Fleer baseball card wrapper. What year is it?

It's from 1963, and as wrappers go, it's quite scarce.

I have a black-and-white postcard-size card of Brooks Robinson with a box of statistics on the back. I have been unable to determine where it is from. Can you help?

Your card is known as a Statistic Back Exhibit. It was part of a 64-card issue in 1963 from the Exhibit Supply Co. The company also did a stat-back set in 1962, with 32 cards. The stats on back are red in the 1962 set, black in 1963. Common cards each year are worth $2-$3, with Hall of Famers worth between $4-$30, and Mantle, between $60-$100.

At a show, I saw a 1967 Topps Roger Maris card with the team name "Yankees" on the bottom. My 1967 Maris has the same photo, but the team name is "Cardinals." I haven't been able to find any information on this discrepancy. Can you shed

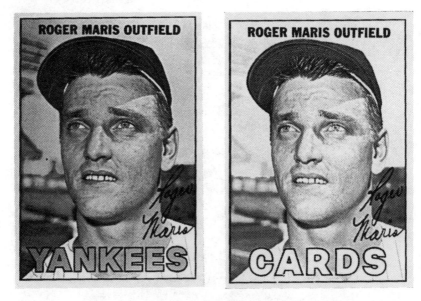

some light on it?

The Maris "Yankee" card is an unissued proof card, prepared by Topps prior to Maris' trade to the Cardinals in December 1966. The blank-backed 1967 Maris Yankees card is the most common proof card in the hobby. An estimated several hundred of them were printed and released through a former Topps executive. The normal "Cardinals" version is a $40 card; the proof sells for around $750.

I have a Topps baseball stamp album and record book with most of the stamps. I think it is a 1962 book because it still has the Houston Colts. Is this book rare? Are there other stamp books of the 1960s?

Topps had stamp sets as wax pack inserts in 1961 (208 brown or green stamps), 1962 (200 color stamps), and 1969 (240 color stamps). Both stamps and albums are quite scarce, but there are few interested collectors, so prices remain low. The whole set from 1962 is valued at $220 in top shape, with $35 for the album.

I have a card that looks like a playing card. The face of the card has Mickey Mantle on it, with the words "Single Runners Advance 2 Bases." What is it?

Your card is part of a 33-card set produced by Topps in 1968. The set was designed to be used as a game based on the situation of each card. The cards, which measure 2¼" by 3¼", were inserted into packs of regular issue 1968 cards or were available as a complete boxed set. The value of this set is $50, with Mantle being the highest priced at $15.

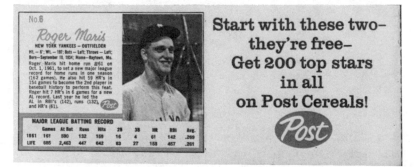

My friend and I have a bet. I say Post Cereal once printed a set of baseball cards;

Card Identifications

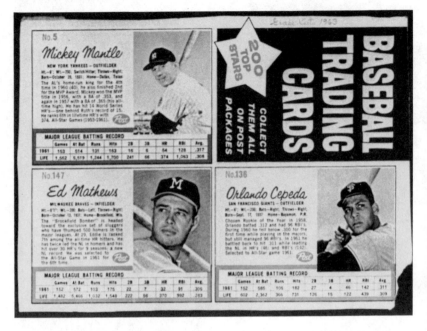

my friend said the company didn't. Who's right?

Baseball cards were put on the backs of Post cereal boxes from 1960-1963. The 1960 set had nine cards, including five baseball players, and measured 7" by 8¾"; the 1961-1963 sets contained 200 cards each, were horizontal and measured (2½" by 3½"). Post cards are very popular among collectors today. Post also produced cards in 1990 and 1991.

I have some cards with cartoons on the front. On the back it says the cards were produced by the Fleer Corp. in 1968. What can you tell me about them?

You have something about which we get a lot of questions. They are Fleer World Series cards. Three sets of these cards were issued in 1968, 1970 and 1971. The 1968 cards are a test issue and carry a 1967 copyright. There are 64 cards in

the 1970 issue and 66 in the 1971 issue. Your cards are from 1970.

Each card has a cartoon illustration and a description of one year's World Series. Each set contains a card from each World Series. Neither set is scarce by any means. Because they don't show pictures of actual players, they're not much in demand, either. The sets go for about $15 apiece, but you can find single cards for around a nickel. And they're a great way to learn about World Series history.

On the back of some Topps cards there are puzzles: 1968 and 1969 Sporting News

All-Stars and 1972 regular cards. Can you tell me what players are on the back of these cards and their numbers?

Carl Yastrzemski is on the back of the 1968 Topps cards #361-380, and again in 1969, cards #416-425. Pete Rose is the puzzle on the backs of 1969 cards #426-435. Yaz is back in 1972, on cards #556, 558, 560, 562, 564, and 570; Joe Torre joins him, on cards #552, 554, 566, 568, 572, and 574; and Tony Oliva is on cards #698, 702, 704, 708, 712, and 714.

I have a Pete Rose card with scalloped edges. Who issued the card? When? And are the edges supposed to be scalloped?

You have a 1969 Topps "deckle edge" card, and the scalloped edges were intentional. They were inserted into some packs of regular 1969 cards. While the

70

card back says only 33 were issued, there were two cards each of #11 and #22, Hoyt Wilhelm and Jim Wynn, and Rusty Staub and Joe Foy, respectively. Commons sell for 25-50 cents. The biggest superstars bring only $7-$10 in top grade; the whole set is valued at $100.

I have some cards I think are from the early 1970s. They are made of paper, in black-and-white, with nothing on the back. The player pictures on front have numbers and symbols (clubs, spades, hearts, diamonds) in the corner, like a deck of playing cards. They measure 1⅝" by 2¼".

Your cards were issued in 1969 by the Globe Import Co. Complete decks can be found at shows for $1-$2.

I have a few questions about the 1969 and 1970 Milton Bradley game cards. How many cards are in each set? Are they valuable? How scarce are they?

The 1969 set has 296 cards and is valued at $500. The 1970 set contains 28 cards and is priced at $300. The 1972 set has 372 cards and is valued at $600. The 1984 set has 30 cards and is priced at $10.

The cards are not all that common, but they aren't worth that much, either. Team insignias are airbrushed or blacked-out on the cards and limits their appeal to team collectors. The big stars are on the want lists of some superstar collectors for a few dollars apiece, but common cards can be found for a quarter or less.

1970-1979 Cards

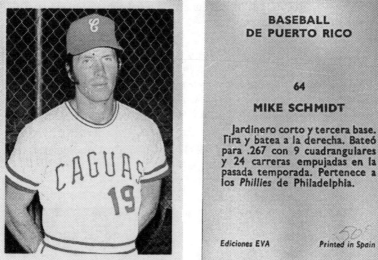

BASEBALL
DE PUERTO RICO

64

MIKE SCHMIDT

Jardinero corto y tercera base. Tira y batea a la derecha. Bateó para .267 con 9 cuadrangulares y 24 carreras empujadas en la pasada temporada. Pertenece a los *Phillies* de Philadelphia.

Ediciones EVA   Printed in Spain

I recently saw an ad featuring a 1970s minor league set with Mike Schmidt for a very hefty price. Does such a set really exist? From what manufacturer?

It's not a minor league set, really. In 1972, Schmidt was pictured on a set of stickers, printed in Puerto Rico, depicting players in the winter league there. The Schmidt sticker is easily worth $200.

I have some Topps baseball scratch-off game cards. Could you give me information about them?

Topps produced scratch-off game cards as inserts in 1970 (white center) and 1971 (red center). There were 24 cards, the same 24 each year, featuring six Hall

of Famers. A separate set of 108 single-player stratch-off cards was issued in 1981. None of the scratch-off cards are popular. Those with the game pieces actually scratched off are virtually worthless.

I remember baseball cards on Milk Duds boxes. What can you tell me about them?

In 1971, 37 National League and 32 American League players cards were printed on 5-cent boxes of Milk Duds. Most collectors prefer to collect the set in complete box form. The set is valued at $1,000 in Near Mint condition.

I received some 8" by 10" Pittsburgh Pirates baseball cards. They have an Arco trademark and Major League Baseball trademark on the back, with the copyright date of 1971. The front has a player photo without a cap. Can you give me some details on these?

These pictures were given away at Arco gas stations for gas purchases in 1971. At the end of the promotion, complete sets were sold for $1 each. There were 12 players each issued for the Red Sox, Pirates and Yankees, and 13 for the Phillies. They remain quite inexpensive today because of lack of collector demand for oversize cards.

I have a card of Johnny Bench (#29), and Rich Allen (#44). They resemble the 1971 Bazooka cards with a couple of differences: 1) The '71 Bazooka set is unnumbered, and, 2) the '71 Bazooka set contains 36 cards, not 48. Are these cards a variation of the '71 Bazookas? Are they scarce?

Your cards are indeed a variation of the 1971 Bazookas. A numbered set of 48 cards was prepared in proof or test issue form, but never issued. They are quite scarce and expensive, and very much in demand by superstar collectors.

Card Identifications

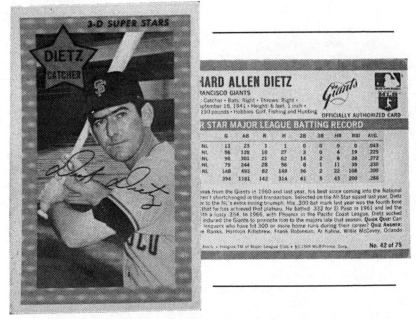

I was sorting through an old box of cards and found a Richard Dietz card that looks like a miniature Sportflics card. On the back is says "1972 Xograph 9 of 54". What is it?

Your card is from the 1972 Kellogg's cereal set. Kellogg's issued 3-D cards between 1970 and 1983, available in cereal boxes and or by mail-in offers.

I have a puzzle that features Dick Allen. Do you have any information on it?

You have one of 12 player jigsaw puzzles issued by Topps in 1974. The 40-piece puzzles came in individual wrappers and never really caught on with collectors.

What can you tell me about the 1973 Topps Team Checklists set?

The Team Checklist set consists of 254 unnumbered cards. The fronts contain facsimilie autographs of players on a given team, while the backs have a team checklist of players in the 1973 Topps set. The cards are somewhat scarce and are believed to be issued as inserts in the high-numbered series of 1973 Topps baseball packs. There is also a 1974 Topps Team Checklists set which is significantly more common than the 1973 set. Unmarked 1973 cards are valued at $2.50 each, while the 1974 cards are priced at 50 cents each.

I came across a few 1975 Topps cards and noticed that some of them are much smaller. What kind of cards are these?

Your smaller versions are known in the hobby as "minis," and they are 20 percent smaller than the regular issue 1975 Topps cards. They were a test issue

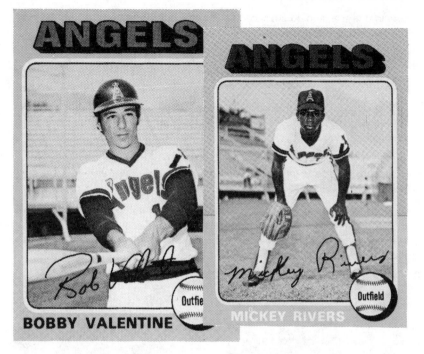

BOBBY VALENTINE

MICKEY RIVERS

to see if kids would buy smaller cards so that Topps could print more cards on a press sheet and save some money. The test never had a chance, because collectors in Michigan and on the West Coast, where the cards were distributed, bought them all up. The 1975 minis are very popular among collectors today.

I have 40-Plus cards of SSPC which I can't find in any guides. They seem to be mostly stars — Mays, Seaver, Yaz, etc. I would like to know more about them.

You really don't have cards from a set. What you have are examples of Sport Star Publishing Co. issues from several sources. SSPC cards were included in the late-1970s in several yearbook-type magazines for some of the more popular East Coast teams — Yankees, Mets, Phillies, and so on — and there were also SSPC cards inserted into a short-lived card collector's magazine of that era.

A friend bought me a set of six Red Sox cards with a 1975 A.L. Champions logo in the lower left corner. The bottom right corner has a "Pee Wee" logo. The cards are numbered 102-107 and the backs have pictures of old cars. Each card is 3" by 5". Can you give me more information on them?

Your cards are from a 36-card 1976 set featuring 12 players from the Reds, Red Sox and Dodgers. The cards were issued in panels of six. The drawings are the work of Massachusetts artist Charles Linnett. Because the cards are non-

Card Identifications

standard in size, and do not show the player's uniform or cap, they are not very popular with collectors. The complete set of 36 can be had for $5-$10.

I have a Topps card, copyright 1976, of Joe Garagiola. It looks like a 1973 Topps card. The back has his address and his phone number at NBC. What is it?

It's Garagiola's former business card. He handed them out fairly liberally, and often autographed them. A similar card was produced for then-Commissioner of Baseball, Bowie Kuhn.

I bought some baseball player discs recently. The dealer said they were issued by Burger King. What can you tell me about them?

Your discs are from a set of 216 different discs that were on Burger King Funmeal boxes in 1977. Like other discs, these are not popular with collectors. A complete set of Funmeal boxes is valued at $35. A set of individual stars detached from the boxes lists at $15.

I purchased 70 cards from what appears to be 1976. They are discs, with the front design in the form of a baseball. All 70 players have airbrushed caps. On the back it has the Crane Potato Chip logo. Do I have a complete set?

Yes, the set is complete at 70. In addition to the Crane's version, these discs can be found with other advertisers' messages on the backs.

I ran across some 1977 Topps cards that are made from a fabric instead of cardboard. What do you know about them?

These are a Topps specialty issue known as "cloth stickers." There were 73 pieces in the set. The backing of the stickers could be taken off and the stickers adhered to a jacket or notebook.

Can you identify a Willie Stargell card #11 I have. It has statistics through the 1977 season and looks like it was cut from a box.

Your card was cut from a three-card panel of Hostess snack products in 1978. There were 150 cards (50 panels) in that set. Hostess produced these cards in panels from 1975-1979.

I bought two comics which featured Jim Rice and Eddie Murray. What can you tell me about these?

These 3" by 3¾" comics were a test issue from Topps in 1979. The comics are actually wax wrappers for a piece of gum. A total of 33 comics make up the set. This issue was bought up in great quantities by speculators and remains rather common today. It is also unpopular because of its comic-style player representations.

Card Identifications

I have several cards that measure 4" by 6" and feature all types of sports stars from baseball, tennis, golf, table tennis, lacrosse, jai alai, etc. They have printed dates of 1977, 1978 or 1979 and say "Editions Rencontre S.A., Lausane" or "Edito-Services S.A., Geneva" and are printed in either Italy or Japan. Can you please acquaint me with what I've got?

You've got what are known as "Sportscaster" cards. They were sold in monthly 24-card packages to subscribers. Some 2,000 different subjects are known, ranging from dozens of worldwide sports. The only cards with much collector value are the 140 baseball subjects, which are valued between 50 cents and $15 in top grade, depending on who is pictured.

1980-Present Cards

I have three baseball "credit cards" of Pete Rose, 1981-1983, made by Perma-Graphics. Could you give me any information on them? I would like to find more, but haven't seen them advertised.

There were six series of Perma-Graphic plastic cards issued between 1981-1983. Each year saw production of a Superstar series and a "gold" All-Star series of between 18-36 cards each. Photos for the cards came from Topps. The cards never really caught on with collectors and are relatively inexpensive today — if you can find them. They are much scarcer than their price tags would dictate.

What puzzles has Donruss included with its baseball cards?

There was no puzzle in 1981; those cards came with bubble gum. The puzzles have been: 1982 — Babe Ruth; 1983 — Ty Cobb; 1984 — Duke Snider; 1985

Lou Gehrig; 1986 — Hank Aaron; 1987 — Roberto Clemente; 1988 — Stan Musial; 1989 — Warren Spahn; 1990 — Carl Yastrzemski; 1991 — Willie Stargell.

I have a 1981 Carl Yastrzemski card which is valued at $1.50. In a card shop, I saw the same card with a Coke logo on it and a price tag of $10. Is this Coke card something special or was the price a fake?

Topps produced 12-card sets for 11 major league teams in 1981. They had the Coca-Cola logos on the front and back. The Yaz Coke card is valued at $1.50. The card dealer is free to price as he wishes. You are free to just say no to ridiculous prices.

I have seven baseball cards issued by Donruss in 1985, each card measuring 3½" by 5". Could you give me more information on these cards?

The cards are part of the 1985 Donruss Action All-Stars set. A complete 60-card set is valued at $8.

I bought a Ryne Sandberg card at a show. It's printed on paper and has his 1983 Topps rookie card on one side, and his 1989 Topps card on the other. It measures 1⅞" by 2½". There were other players such as Mike Greenwell, too. I have a feeling it's counterfeit. Am I correct?

No. What you have is the paper insert that someone broke out of the plastic stand from a 1989 Topps "Doubleheader." While the Doubleheaders may or may not turn out to have been a scarce test issue, without the plastic frame your Sandberg is valueless.

79

Card Identifications

I got four baseball cards from friends. They are Steve Garvey, Graig Nettles, Ray Knight and Gary Matthews. On the front they show a picture of the player and say "Louisville Slugger." What year are they? How many are in the series? Are they worth anything?

These are called "glove hanger cards." They came attached to baseball gloves in stores — that explains the hole punched in the left-hand corner. They were issued in the 1980s with Louisville Slugger and other brands of gloves. There is no complete checklist, and we understand that some player/team variations are quite rare. Values seem to range from less than $1 to $5, depending on player and condition.

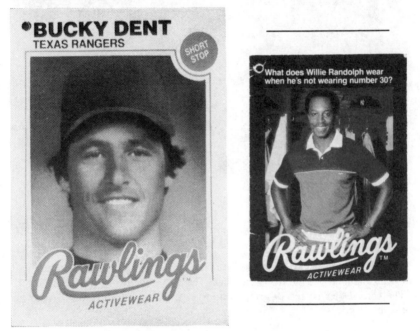

Several years ago, my wife bought my son some clothing with a "fold-open" card of Bucky Dent. I also found a similar card of Nolan Ryan. These cards were printed by Rawlings Activewear. I wrote Rawlings, but they could give no help. Do you know what other players are in this set?

Besides the two you mentioned, there is Willie Randolph, Tom Seaver and former Oakland Raiders punter Ray Guy. The cards date from 1983, and there are two cards for each player — one picturing him in uniform, the other in the company's leisure wear.

I have enclosed several pictures of a set of cards I purchased. They are 1½" by 2½" with blank backs. I was informed they were a Donruss prototype sheet, issued at a card show in 1989. Do they have any value in their present state? How many cards were in a sheet? Were these cards issued with serial numbers? Are they rare and worth keeping?

Your "cards" were cut off a souvenir sheet given away at the Upper Deck booth during the 1989 Chicago National Sports Collectors Convention. There were eight photos of 1989 Upper Deck cards reproduced on the sheet, which carried a red serial number in the lower right-hand corner. While the sheets themselves sell for $10-$20 each, the "cards" cut from them are worthless.

I purchased a "factory sealed" version of the 1984 Donruss set. I was wondering, in this set version, which of the Mike Stenhouse and Ron Darling variations are included? Are the "A" and "B" Living Legends cards included?

The 1984 Donruss factory set has the Darling and Stenhouse cards with numbers. The Living Legends cards were found only in wax packs.

I found some Donruss cards that measure 3½" by 5". Some of the cards are drawings of Hall of Famers. Others are pictures of recent players. I think they are from 1984. What do you know about them?

They're from the 1984 60-card Donruss Champions set. It consists of 49 cards showing action shots of modern players, 10 cards showing Hall of Famers (called "Grand Champions"), and a checklist. The cards are plentiful and inexpensive.

I have a handful of 1984 Topps rub downs. Was this the first and only year they were made?

No. Topps also produced 32-sheet sets of rub downs (pictures on a sheet that can be transfered to another surface by rubbing the paper backing) in 1985. They are scarce as Topps specialty items go, but there is no collector demand for

Card Identifications

them, so the value has remained low. Topps first used the "Magic Rub-Off" idea in 1961, with a 36-piece set that is also scarce, but unpopular.

I purchased a boxed set called "All-Time Record Holders," which is identical to the 1985 Woolworth set, although the box it came in is different. What can you tell me about this set?

What you have are "leftover" Woolworth cards repackaged in a new box.

I saw a dealer advertising 1984 Nestles which looked almost exactly like the 1984 Topps issue. The Nestles cards my brother and I have, however, are very different. Could you tell us what we have here?

Nestle issued two sets in 1984. The most well-known set is the Topps Nestles set (a mail-in premium offer) where the cards — uncut sheets, actually — look exactly like the regular 1984 Topps cards except for the Nestle logo. The other 1984 Nestle set, the "Dream Team" set, was also issued by Topps. The 22-card set is vastly different from the regular 1984 set, and was issued in individual cards as opposed to uncut sheets.

I buy Donruss sets every year. Some cards just say "Donruss" on the back, others say "Donruss-Leaf." Would you explain the difference in these sets?

Through the 1985 issue, Donruss cards carried the "Donruss" copyright on the back. In 1986, the copyright changed to "Leaf-Donruss," and since 1987, it has been "Leaf." This merely reflects the change in corporate ownership of the company which makes Donruss cards. However, when the word "Leaf" is found on the front of the cards (1986-1988), or there is a bright green leaf symbol on the front (1985), this indicates the special Canadian issue made by Donruss.

I have several 1984 Topps cards. Where the Topps logo on the front of the card is supposed to be, it says "O-Pee-Chee." What does that mean? Are they worthless?

It means your cards are the Canadian version of the Topps issue, which were sold in Canada under the O-Pee-Chee brand name. They are generally valued about the same as corresponding Topps cards, although big stars and hot rookies might be valued a bit more. O-Pee-Chee has produced cards since 1965.

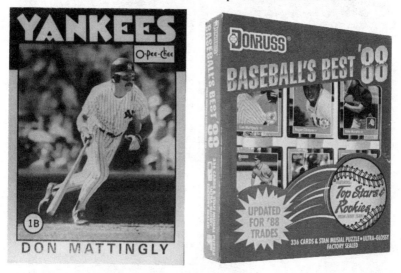

I have a 1988 Donruss Leaf set that is orange. Could you tell me how much it is worth?

The 6th edition of the Sports Collectors Digest Baseball Card Price Guide annual says it is an $18 set, but if you look around you can find it for $15 or less. You have the year-end "Baseball's Best" set. Donruss issued a similar set in 1989, and separate sets for each league in 1990. Collectors don't seem to like them much.

I bought a set of 10 "Weis Winners" discs with pictures and stats on them. What are they?

The discs, officially known as Baseball Super Stars discs, were produced by Michael Schechter and Associates (hence the air-brushed hats and familiar-looking photos). The discs were inserted into canisters of iced-tea mix around the country. Distribution was limited to regional grocery-store chains. In addition to the Weis chain, discs were produced for the Acme, Alpha Beta, Bustelo,

Card Identifications

Key, King Kullen, Lade Lee and Our Own grocery chains.

Discs were not produced in equal quantities for different chains, so discs from some chains are rarer than others. The 20 discs came in 10 two-disc panels. Each panel also had a mail-in offer disc. A Mint set in panel form is valued at $6, and $2 in separated form. Sets from scarcer stores have accordingly higher values.

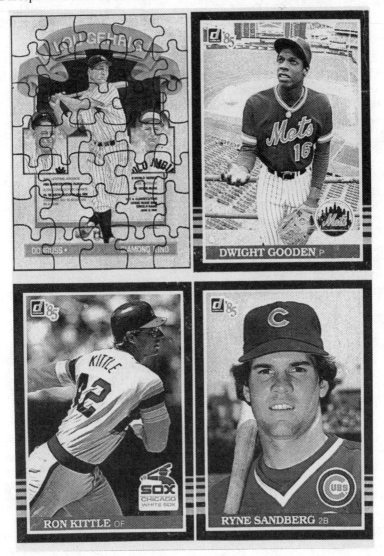

I have a 1985 Donruss Dwight Gooden numbered PC1. I would like to know what type of card this is.

It's a Donruss box panel card. Ron Kittle and Ryne Sandberg were also on the panels. The Gooden card catalogs for $6.50 in Near Mint condition.

I have two "Two for the Title" cards featuring Don Mattingly and Dave Winfield. One card is #651 and the other #140, but they're almost identical in all other respects. I'm confused!

Card #651 is from the 1985 Donruss set. The other (#140) is part of the 264-card 1985 Leaf Donruss set which was sold in Canada. The value of the Leaf-Donruss card is slightly less than the regular Donruss version.

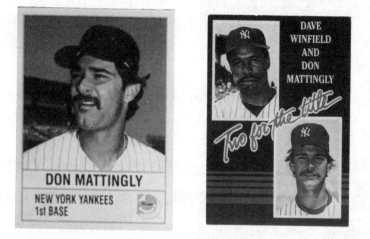

As I was going through my cards, I found a Don Mattingly card issued by a company called Dorman's. Can you give me some information on it?

Dorman cards were produced in 1986 with a total of 20 cards. One of 10 two-card panels were inserted into packages of Dorman's cheese slices. This is one of the 1986 issues that didn't fall into dealer hands in any great number, so the cards are somewhat scarce.

I have a complete set of 20 1985 Kitty Clover discs. They are not numbered and are the same size as Jiffy Pop discs. How and when were these distributed? Are they scarce?

The discs were distributed in bags of Kitty Clover Potato Chips around Missouri and Kansas, and possibly into Nebraska and Iowa. Are they scarce? Yes, compared to 1985 Topps cards, and yes, compared to other 1985 disc sets. But collectors don't care that much for discs and values reflect that.

I want to know if the Big League Chew company ever offered baseball cards.

Yes. In 1986, the shredded bubble gum contained one of 12 "Home Run Legends" cards in each pack, which also had a write-in offer. The cards are of players with 500 or more home runs at the time.

Card Identifications

I have two 1986 Topps Wade Boggs cards. One is #510, while the other has the letter "B." It must be an error.

Neither card is an error. The second card you mention is a Topps box-bottom card.

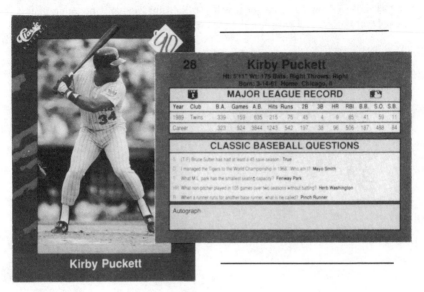

Kirby Puckett

I bought a set of 50 baseball cards called "Classic Baseball." It has all the major stars. I was wondering the nature of these cards.

The Classic cards have been produced since 1987. The original set of 100 cards came with a boxed trivia board game. So-called "travel edition" sets have been issued since then to update the game. The 1987 issues were by Game Time Ltd. In 1988, a card dealer bought the rights to the game and has issued several new series. These cards seem to have found their niche in the hobby.

I have three unusual 1986 Sportflics cards. There is a Pete Rose, #43 (he should be #50); a Tom Seaver, #45 (he should be #25); and a Tri-Star with Schmidt, Murphy and Rice which is not on the 1986 checklist at all. Also, the stats on the back stop at 1984. What can you tell me about them?

You have three of the 1984 Sportflics "test issue" cards, distributed to prospective wholesalers in late 1985 to determine their interest in the coming 1986 set. Because the photos on the cards are also different from the regular-issue 1986 Sportflics, these are quite popular with collectors. We've seen the Rose sell for $20, the Seaver and Tri-Star for half of that.

I have a 1987 Donruss Bo Jackson with a purple border instead of the usual black. Plus, the card number on the back is #205 instead of #35. Could you explain this to me?

Your Jackson card is from the 272-card 1987 Donruss Opening Day set. The card fronts are identical in design to the regular issue Donruss except for the color of the border.

My 1988 Donruss checklist (#600) has 26 cards that have a "BC" in front of the card number. However, I've never seen these cards. What's going on?

The 1988 Donruss MVP cards were randomly inserted in wax and rack packs. So unless you completed your set by buying packs, you wouldn't have received any of the bonus cards numbered BC-1 to BC-26.

I have a 1989 Topps card of Bruce Sutter. On the back, where the number should be, there is an "M." What does this mean?

It means the card was one of 16 printed on the bottoms of Topps wax boxes. Most collectors value them about the same as the player's regular Topps card, although they are much rarer, especially in Mint condition.

I have three 1988 Donruss cards of Kirby Puckett without #368 on the back. Is this an error? Are these cards of any additional value?

It's not an error, but the cards may have some premium value. The no-number Puckett card was printed on the backs of some 1988 Donruss "super-rack" packages. They are quite scarce, but since most people are unaware of them, the price hasn't gone up — yet.

I have a sample pack of cards marked "Series No. 1 Action Packed" copyright 1987 by Hi-Pro Marketing Inc. The cards are of Don Mattingly, Dwight Gooden, Carney Lansford, Andre Dawson and Wade Boggs. The cards have a gold border and the actual pictures of the players are raised (embossed) on the cards. On the backs is a smaller color picture and the player and his stats. What can you tell me about the set?

Card Identifications

The company produced these samples in hopes of getting a license from Major League Baseball to do a set. It did not get a license, so these samples are technically unauthorized collector issues. The company has produced sets of football cards in 1989-91, similar to the 1987 baseball card design.

Enclosed is a 1991 Topps Operation Desert Storm card that is probably a piece of history. My son, who was in the Persian Gulf War, sent me some of these cards. I have been going to card shows and dealers to find out what they are worth. A few dealers have been trading with me and allowing me $3 to $5 for the commons. Can you please tell me if they are worth more and how many were sent over to our boys? I've heard sets were selling for $5,000 and that less than 5,000 cards of each player were produced, but I don't think that all the cards that were sent will come back. Do you think I should save them or keep trading?

The "Desert Shield" gold-embossed Topps cards have become quite popular with collectors. According to Topps, some five million cards were made — enough to make 6,300 sets, if an equal number of each card was made. Not all of the cards were shipped to the Mideast; some were given to the troops upon their return to the United States. Current retail value for commons is about $5, with superstars and hot rookies bringing up to $100 to $300 each. Someone has started counterfeiting the embossed logo, so collectors have had to become wary of fakes, which may eventually hurt the market for the genuine cards. It is our opinion that the value of these novelty cards has peaked; there is little room for future appreciation. Already, the retail price for complete sets has dropped from $10,000 to $4,500.

The 1989 Fleer card of Pete Stanicek has something written on the end of his bat knob. Since the Billy Ripken card had an obscenity, I started to look at the other cards, but I can't read it. Could you tell me what it is?

It says "Stano," his nickname.

88

Major Card Issues

1948 Bowman

1949 Bowman

1950 Bowman

1951 Bowman

1952 Bowman

1953 Bowman Black & White

1953 Bowman Color

1954 Bowman

1955 Bowman

Major Card Issues

1989 Bowman

1990 Bowman

1991 Bowman

1952 Topps

1953 Topps

1954 Topps

1955 Topps

1956 Topps

1957 Topps

Major Card Issues

1958 Topps

1959 Topps

1960 Topps

1961 Topps

1962 Topps

1963 Topps

1964 Topps

1965 Topps

1966 Topps

Major Card Issues

1967 Topps

1968 Topps

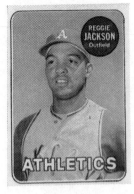

1969 Topps

1970 Topps

1971 Topps

1972 Topps

1973 Topps

1974 Topps

1975 Topps

Major Card Issues

1976 Topps

1977 Topps

1978 Topps

1979 Topps

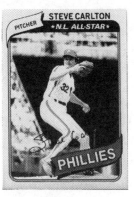
1980 Topps

1981 Topps

1982 Topps

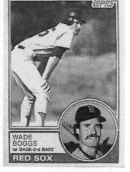
1983 Topps

1984 Topps

Major Card Issues

1985 Topps

1986 Topps

1987 Topps

1988 Topps

1989 Topps

1990 Topps

1991 Topps

1991 Topps Stadium Club

1963 Fleer

Major Card Issues

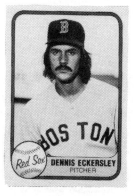
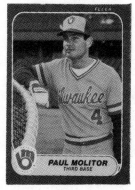

1981 Fleer	1982 Fleer	1983 Fleer
1984 Fleer	1985 Fleer	1986 Fleer
1987 Fleer	1988 Fleer	1989 Fleer

Major Card Issues

1990 Fleer

1991 Fleer

1991 Fleer Ultra

1981 Donruss

1982 Donruss

1983 Donruss

1984 Donruss

1985 Donruss

1986 Donruss

Major Card Issues

1987 Donruss

1988 Donruss

1989 Donruss

1990 Donruss

1991 Donruss

1991 Donruss Studio

1988 Score

1989 Score

1990 Score

Major Card Issues

1991 Score

Roger Clemens

1989 Upper Deck

Gregg Jefferies

1990 Upper Deck

Ozzie Smith

1991 Upper Deck

1986 Sportflics

1987 Sportflics

1988 Sportflics

1989 Sportflics

1990 Sportflics

The Five Ws
of
Baseball Cards

Chapter Four

Who, What, Why, Where & When

Is there a book that lists all of the cards made of a certain player?

I suggest you purchase a copy of the *Sport Americana Baseball Card Alphabetical Checklist*. It lists the major baseball card sets in which a player was included.

What are the addresses of the baseball card companies?

Topps Chewing Gum Co./Bowman, 254 36th St., Brooklyn, N.Y. 11232.

Fleer Corp., Executive Plaza, Suite 300, 1120 Route 73, Mount Laurel, N.J. 08054.

Leaf-Donruss Co., 975 Kansas St, Memphis, Tenn. 38101.

Sportflics/Score, Major League Marketing Inc., 25 Ford Road, Westport, Conn. 06880.

Upper Deck Co., 1174 N. Grove St., Anaheim, Calif. 92806.

What is the mailing address of the Baseball Hall of Fame?

National Baseball Hall of Fame and Museum, P.O. Box 590, Cooperstown, N.Y. 13326.

The Five Ws of Baseball Cards

We are having trouble getting our collection insured. All the agents we called said they could not give us a special rider for our home owner policy to cover our cards. As it now stands, if the cards were stolen or burned, we'd only get 45 cents per 15 cards. Can you put us in contact with someone who can help?

An Ohio firm that has offered card collector's insurance for a number of years is Cornell & Finklemeir. Contact the agency at P.O. Box 210, Wapkoneta, Ohio 45895.

I've heard of a company that will print baseball cards of anybody, if you send your picture and information. Do you have further information?

Several companies produce custom cards, as you've described. The biggest manufacturer is former Yankees pitcher Jim Bouton, of Big League Cards, P.O. Box C, Teaneck, N.J. 07666. Another company is called Unbeatables, which can be reached at P.O. Box 187, Glenville Station, Greenwich, Conn. 06831-0887.

Why is Topps the only company to put gum in its card packs?

Topps has an exclusive contract with Major League Baseball and the players' association to market baseball cards with gum or other "confectionery" products. That contract is up for renewal soon, and you can bet the other gum companies may be bidding for those rights.

How many 792-card sets does Topps produce each year?

Card companies won't release those figures, citing competitive pressure as the reason. It is our informed estimate that Topps is currently producing more than 3,000,000 cards of each player in its regular set each year.

Do card companies produce fewer cards of the star players than of the common players?

In most sets produced today, the major card companies produce exactly the same number of each card.

Why aren't Topps cards put in any order?

Topps (and Upper Deck, Sportflics, Donruss and Score) cards are in order — numerical order. But you're right in describing the numerical order as absolutely random. The numbers don't mean anything — unlike Fleer numbers, which place a player with a team, and a team within last year's overall standings. If you keep cards in team order, which makes sense, or in numerical order, which also makes sense, it makes a lot more sense to number cards by team. Topps did it with its football cards in the 1960s, and O-Pee-Chee occasionally does it with hockey, but we can't understand why it's not done more.

The 1990 Fleer factory-sealed set that I received at Christmas had the cards all out of numerical order. Could this set have been tampered with?

No. Fleer factory sets are not arranged in numerical order when they are packaged.

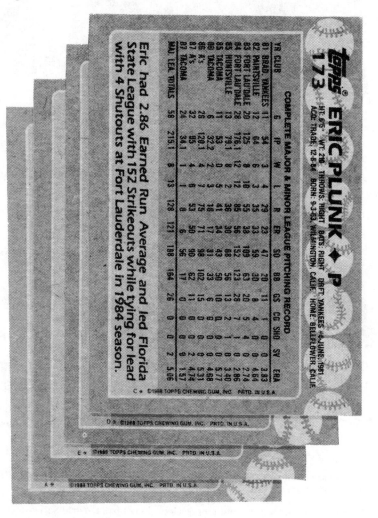

What does the small letter — A, B, C, D, E or F — on the back of a Topps card mean?

It indicates on which of the 132-card sheets the card was printed.

Why do card companies print cards of players who have not played in the major leagues yet?

To get a competitive edge. The card companies are as conscious as everybody else about the demand for rookie cards.

I would like to know why Topps, Fleer, Donruss and the other companies don't print playoff or World Series cards. I always enjoy looking at such cards and remembering the great games.

Although Topps, Donruss and Upper Deck do not print World Series or play-off cards, Fleer and Score do. Fleer's cards are found only in its factory sets; Score prints its card as part of the regular set. One reason the other companies don't print these cards is because their next year's card sets are usually ready for the press by the time the Series is complete.

DeWAYNE BUICE

I have a question about the 1988 Upper Deck promotional cards. The only ones advertised are Wally Joyner and DeWayne Buice. Why hasn't anyone found the Gary Pettis card? I know it exists because it's pictured on the front of his 1989 Upper Deck card, #117.

That's trick photography at work. Upper Deck shot Pettis holding a blank card front, then worked the finished card back over the blank card on the card front.

Gary Pettis KEN GRIFFEY, JR OF

*I've seen your monthly **Baseball Card Price Guide** show a picture of a 1990 Leaf card of Joe Carter that is a different picture than my Joe Carter Leaf card. Is the one in your magazine a "promo" card? If so, where can I get one?*

We've pictured a promo card of Joe Carter. In addition to the Carter promo, Leaf produced sample cards of Eric Anthony, Robin Ventura, Greg Vaughn, Bobby Bonilla, Gary Gaetti, Ozzie Smith, Steve Sax, Dennis Eckersley, Ken Griffey Jr., Barry Larkin and Mark Langston. Donruss sent two of the cards to each dealer in its distribution network and these are the source of the cards seen in the ads and at shows. A typical Leaf promo card sells between $50-$100.

103

The Five Ws of Baseball Cards

When baseball card companies print "limited-edition" sets, who governs just how many they make? Who makes sure they only print that limited number? Do they do it on the honor system or what?

There is no definition of "limited edition." To some card companies that means 10,000, to some it means 100,000. There is no watchdog overseeing the print run, so the hobby has to take the manufacturer's word on production numbers.

Can you tell me about what time of year gum companies announce their sets for the following season? Also, do you know when each company knows what player will be given a designated number for that set?

Generally, by the time the last pitch is thrown in the World Series, the card companies are well on their way to organizing the coming year's sets. By November, checklists are usually completed, and announcement of availability is made to dealers.

When I go to card stores I sometimes see that they have prototype cards of various companies. I have always wondered from where and how they get them, if I can get any, and how.

The large-scale use of prototype or sample cards by manufacturers to get retailers interested in their new products is a fairly new phenomenon, begun by Sportflics in 1985. Originally, the sample cards were intended to give dealers a look at the new product. Today, however, many of the card companies are using prototype cards as ordering bonuses. Prototype cards of popular players in sets can sell for $50-$100 each. At that price, they are a poor investment.

I went to a Kansas City Royals game early in 1991 and they gave away free baseball cards. It was a team set of the Royals, including a Bo Jackson card which is rare. Two weeks later the Kansas City police burned 250,000 of the Bo Jackson cards. Somehow a guy found out I had one extra card. He offered me $125 cash for this card. Should I sell it? Could it ever be a Honus Wagner card?

We won't make a buy-sell recommendation in this column; that has to be your decision. However, if anybody ever offered me $125 for a current-year card that I got for free, I'd sell. If you figure that at least 15,000-25,000 of the sets were probably given away at the game you attended, there's no chance of this card ever becoming another Wagner in terms of rarity.

On the 1988 Topps Brian Horton card, his ERA is listed at 4.19, and his 1988 Donruss card lists it at 4.22. Why the difference?

The difference in ERAs between Topps and Donruss stems from the fact that Donruss drops the fraction of an inning pitched in figuring ERAS, while Topps uses the fractions.

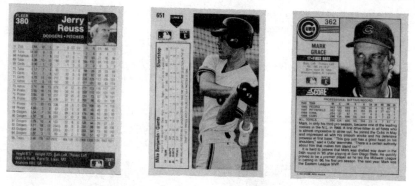

On all 1981 to 1985 Fleer Jerry Reuss cards, the word "Home" is missing from the section on the card back that contains the player's personal data. How could this mistake be made from one year to the next?

The card companies store on computer the statistical and personal information carried on card backs. Unless a mistake is corrected in the computer records, it is repeated each year.

Mark Grace's 1989 Score card says that "in only his third pro season ..." but according to his stats, 1988 was his first year. Why is this?

In baseball, a player is considered a professional at the minor league level since he's getting paid for playing. Minor league players consider it an insult when someone asks them when they're going to get to "the pros."

On the back of the 1991 Upper Deck card of Mike Benjamin (#651), in the 1989 stats it says he had a .167 average, 14 games, six at-bats, six runs, one hit, no doubles, triples, home runs, walks or stolen bases and one strikeout. My question is, how did he score six runs while only getting on base once?

As a pinch runner.

Can you tell me why the backs of some 1954 Topps cards are upside down? This occurs even within the same series or press sheets.

If you'll notice, the 1954 Topps cards have no top border. To achieve this effect, they were printed with one row upside down atop another. When cut apart, half of the cards seem to have backs that are upside down in relation to the fronts.

Why do the Topps 1955 and 1956 cards identify the Washington Senators as "Washington Nationals"? They were not in the National League.

The Five Ws of Baseball Cards

It was a shameless plug for the team's largest advertiser, the National Brewing Co., which sponsored the team's radio broadcasts.

While looking at my older cards, I noticed the 1969 Topps cards have two different backs, some with, and some without, cartoons. Do you know why Topps did this?

Space. If you'll notice, the cards without the cartoons are generally those of older players, and Topps needed extra room for statistics.

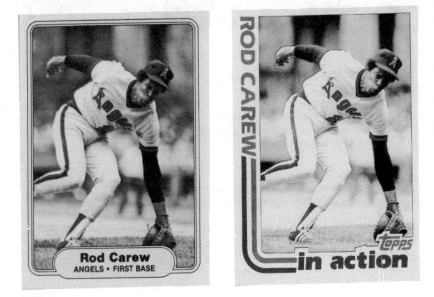

The 1982 Fleer and Topps cards of Rod Carew use the same photo. Has this happened on other cards before?

The Carew coincidence is the first and only time that the same photo has appeared on two different card companies' cards since 1981.

The 1968 and 1969 Topps cards of Carl Yastrzemski have the same picture of him, although the 1969 is blown up somewhat bigger. Why was this done, and do you know of other players that have had the same picture printed on different cards?

It was done for ease, to save a few bucks or just a plain lack of initiative. Topps commonly used the same photo for two or three years back in the 1950s and 1960s. And the same photo was frequently used on different regional issues all the way back to the 1910s.

Why do some of the 1989 Donruss Diamond King cards have crowns on the backs of the card with year dates in them?

106

It indicates the player appeared as a Diamond King in that year's Donruss set.

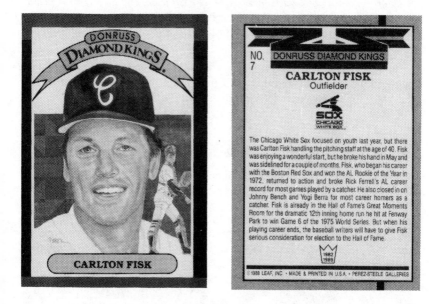

Why does the 1989 Diamond King card of Carlton Fisk say he's an outfielder when on the front he is in catching gear?

Prior to the 1989 season, Donruss guessed Fisk, who had played some in the outfield in 1986-1987, might move out from behind the plate more regularly. It didn't work out that way.

Why does the 1952 Topps reprint set have only 402 cards, as opposed to the 407 in the original issue? If the entire set had been reprinted, I would have probaby bought it.

Topps could not find or obtain permission for the rights to reproduce the cards (a nicety which other card reprinters ignore). The missing five are Solly Hemus, Saul Rogovin, Dom DiMaggio, Tommy Holmes and Billy Loes.

Why don't Topps Traded cards come in wax packs?

They did, on an experimental basis in 1985. The experiment flopped for the same reason Topps stopped producing cards in series in 1974. By late in the baseball season, when the Traded set is released, the average (non-collector) buyer of bubble gum cards wants football cards, not baseball.

The Five Ws of Baseball Cards

I recently purchased an uncut sheet of 27 Topps cards of 1982. The sheet has the 26 batting and pitching leaders' cards, one for each team, and an advertising card offering Topps baseball card collecting boxes for $1 and a wax wrapper. Topps 792-card sets are printed on six sheets of 132 cards each. Where would they find room for these extra 27 cards?

The team leader cards are technically known as "double prints." Topps just packaged them up with the other cards from the regular press sheets. This explains why you find team leader cards so often in 1982 Topps.

I've seen 1953 Topps cards listed as "singleprints." What does this mean?

For most years through 1981, the number of cards in a Topps set and the general configuration of the sheets in which cards were printed meant that certain cards were printed twice on each sheet. Such cards are called "doubleprints" and are twice as common as the rest of the cards on the same sheet. In 1953, there were fewer singleprints than doubleprints, so it makes more sense to list them individually. Because they are twice as rare, they command premium prices.

Why are small sets like the K-Mart and others usually printed in sets of 33 or 44 cards?

Because those numbers are easily divisible into the standard 132-card (12 rows of 11 cards each) sheet on which baseball cards are printed today. An uncut sheet of 33 card sets will yield four compete sets; 44-card sets come three to a sheet.

I was looking through some of my dad's 1954 Bowmans and noticed that Johnny Antonelli (#208) has his name typed and not signed. Why?

Most likely because Bowman did not have a facsimile autograph of Antonelli on file.

What is Chris Sabo holding on his 1990 Fleer card?

It's an on-deck bat. The weights are adjustable to the player's preference.

Why does the 1988 Topps Mark McGwire have an all-star trophy on it?

Topps all-star rookie cards recognize players who were top rookies the year before the cards were issued; they are not necessarily that player's rookie card. So while the 1988 all-star rookie cards of Matt Nokes and Ellis Burks are the rookie cards for those players, McGwire's all-star rookie card is not his rookie card.

The Five Ws of Baseball Cards

Why doesn't Don Mattingly's rookie card appear in the 1983 Topps Traded set along with Darryl Strawberry? Also, why doesn't Roger Clemens' rookie card appear in the 1984 Topps Traded set while Dwight Gooden made the set?

The amount of pre-major league publicity and playing time in those debut seasons seems to be the key. Strawberry and Gooden were much-heralded saviors of the Mets franchise when they were brought up from the minors, while Mattingly and Clemens were relatively unknown. Strawberry came up to New York early enough in 1983 to make the Traded set, playing in 122 games.

Mattingly appeared in only 91 major league games that year, apparently missing the cut-off date. Similarly, in 1984 Gooden played the entire season with the Mets, while Clemens was up and down between Boston and Pawtucket that year. It appears that Topps observes an early June cut-off date for inclusion in each year's Traded set. Clemens did, however, appear in the 1984 Fleer Update set.

Why isn't Howard Johnson's 1985 Topps card his rookie card? It's his first Topps card.

HoJo's rookie cards are in the 1983 Fleer and Donruss sets. By the standard hobby definition of "rookie card," HoJo's 1985 Topps card is not considered his rookie card. Topps missed the boat on HoJo.

Are #1 draft pick cards considered rookie cards?

No. It's a fine distinction, but a card has to be a "regular" card to be a rookie card. Special cards don't count.

110

What is Jose Canseco's Topps rookie card? I've looked everywhere and cannot find it.

Canseco does not have a Topps rookie card. Donruss and Fleer beat Topps to the punch when they issued rookie cards of Canseco in their regular issue 1986 sets. Topps did not produce a regular issue Canseco card until 1987.

Topps did include a Canseco card in its 1986 Topps Traded set. However, the hobby does not recognize a card from a "Traded," "Update" or "Rookies" set to be a true rookie card, since the set was sold only through hobby dealers, and was not nationally distributed to the general public.

The letters (FC) after a card found in the *Sports Card Price Guide Monthly* and annual *Sports Collectors Digest Baseball Card Price Guide,* etc., (including those cards found in Traded and Update sets), indicate a player's first card for that particular company.

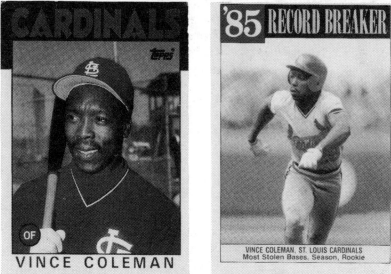

Why isn't Vince Coleman's 1985 Topps Record Breaker card considered his rookie card?

Most collectors feel that only a "regular" card can be considered a player's "real" rookie card.

The Five Ws of Baseball Cards

At a show I bought a 1986 and 1987 Donruss rookie card of Bo Jackson. How could he be a rookie two straight years?

Jackson did not play enough games for the Kansas City Royals in 1986 to lose his rookie status for 1987. Also, Donruss probably figured the inclusion of Jackson in the 1987 set would make it more popular — it turns out Donruss was right.

Kevin Seitzer is in the regular 1987 Fleer set, on card #652. He's also in the 1987 Fleer Update set, card #108. Why is he in both sets?

Because he was a hot rookie in 1987, and Fleer figured it would sell more sets with Seitzer than without him. Also, Seitzer shares his "regular" 1987 Fleer card with another player. It has been Fleer's policy to include players from these "Major League Prospect" cards in its Update sets, as was done with Jose Canseco in 1986 and Mark Grace in 1988, both of whom appeared on a multi-player Major League Prospect card.

Why did Stan Musial's first Topps card appear in 1958, although he had Bowman cards in 1948-1949 and 1952-1953?

He likely felt the gum companies weren't paying him enough. Musial did appear on several national and regional issues in the period from 1952-1955, including Red Man Tobacco, Red Heart Dog Food and Hunter's Hot Dogs.

I noticed Bowman only made Jackie Robinson cards in 1949 and 1950. Why didn't Bowman make cards of him in his other years?

It's assumed Topps signed him to an exclusive contract for 1952 and later. Why Bowman didn't include Robinson in 1948 and 1951 sets is open to speculation.

Why did Donruss make Rated Rookie cards of Danny Tartabull in both 1985 and 1986? Which is his real rookie card?

The real rookie card is 1985. Tartabull spent virtually all of 1985 in the minor leagues, so he was still a rookie in 1986.

Why isn't the 1986 Topps #389 Glenn Davis not his rookie card? This was Davis' first Topps card.

The Five Ws of Baseball Cards

Glenn Davis' rookie card is the 1985 Fleer Major League Prospect card #652 that he shares with Joe Hesketh. The 1986 Topps card is merely his first appearance for Topps, not a true rookie card.

Why do Danny Heep and Bobby Sprowl appear on two consecutive years of Astros Future Stars cards — 1981 (#81) and 1982 (#441)?

It wasn't uncommon for Topps to do that. Some players appeared as rookie prospects in three, four or even five different years.

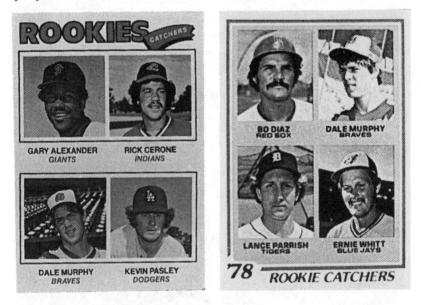

I have Rookie Catchers cards from the 1977 Topps set (#476) and the 1978 Topps set (#708) that include Dale Murphy. Why is Murphy listed as a rookie in two consecutive years?

Murphy, who started his career as a catcher, played parts of 1976 and 1977 with the Atlanta Braves, but not enough to lose his rookie status. He was still considered a rookie when the 1978 season began.

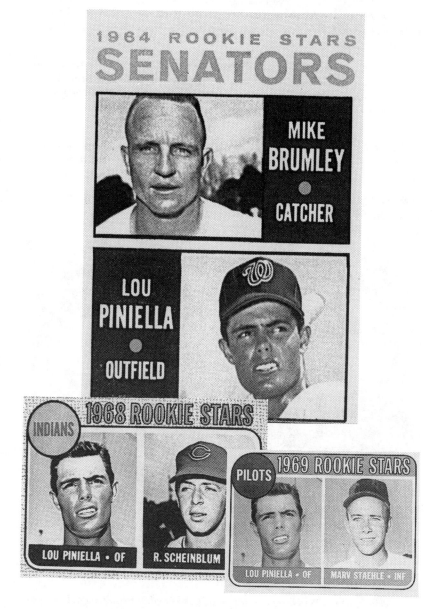

I noticed a listing for a 1964 Senators Rookies card with Lou Piniella. Wasn't Piniella the American League Rookie of the Year with the Kansas City Royals?

Actually, Piniella was featured on three-multiplayer rookie cards, besides the two you mention. Piniella was on an Indians Rookies card in the 1968 Topps set. It was with the Royals in 1969 that Piniella ended his seven-year minor league career and was named A.L. Rookie of the Year.

The Five Ws of Baseball Cards

My brother went to Japan for school this year. I asked him if he would pick up a Cecil Fielder card for me, from when he played with the Hanshin Tigers. How rare is the card here and what is it worth?

There are only one or two issues of baseball cards in Japan each year, the most popular being issued with potato chips. In the past year there have been significant imports of recent Japanese cards into the United States. The Fielder card, however, is more popular enough that it is usually sold for $10 or more.

The 1991 Upper Deck Steve Sax card (#462) shows him jumping over a sliding Atlanta Brave. I don't remember the Yankees playing the Braves. Did they play in spring training or was this photo artificially created?

While Upper Deck has done some wonderous things in creating composite action photos for some of its cards, this particular scene could have been taken at spring training because both clubs play in Florida.

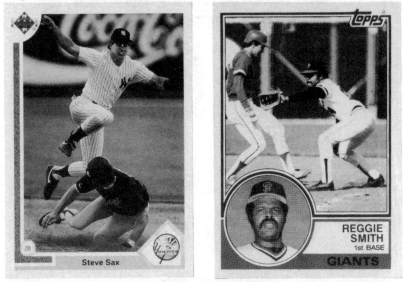

I have a question concerning Reggie Smith's 1983 Topps card (#282). Could you tell me if the Cub pictured with him is Ryne Sandberg? It sure looks like him.

It's Sandberg, making a cameo appearance, but that doesn't add any extra value to the card.

Recent ads for 1988 Olympic team autographs say that Ben McDonald was on this team. Why doesn't the 1988 Topps Traded set have his card?

To avoid violating rules pertaining to amateur status. Topps was able to print cards only of those players on the 1988 USA Olmypic team who were college seniors or otherwise out of collegiate eligibility. McDonald was a junior at Louisiana State University in 1988. The same situation existed in 1985, when Topps was unable to print cards of Will Clark, B.J. Surhoff, Barry Larkin and others on the 1984 team.

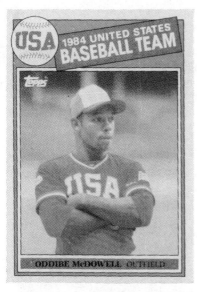
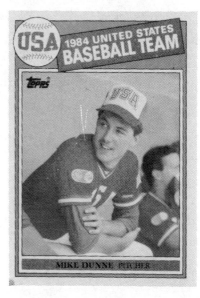

In the 1985 Topps set, why wasn't there a Will Clark Olympic card?

Only the seniors from the Olympic team, or those without further college eligibility, were included in the Topps set. The underclassmen, who still had amateur status, couldn't receive payment for appearing on the cards.

Why isn't Mickey Mantle in the 1955 Topps set? Was he injured or what?

Mantle was not included in the 1954 and 1955 Topps sets because he was signed to an exclusive contract with Bowman. Mantle is card #65 in the 1954 Bowman set, and #202 in the 1955 edition.

Why weren't there any 1972 or 1973 Topps cards of Rusty Staub?

Staub refused to join the players' union during that span so he wasn't allowed to appear on baseball cards. Staub was the most obvious omission over that period, though there were others.

Why doesn't former relief pitcher Mike Marshall appear on any Topps baseball cards from 1978 on?

We'd guess he refused to re-sign his Topps contract when it came due. Marshall is a staunch believer that baseball players should not be treated as heroes, and has long maintained a policy of not signing autographs. Allowing his Topps contract to lapse would be in keeping with that stance. Marshall does appear in the 1982 Fleer set.

The Five Ws of Baseball Cards

Why is Danny Jackson's first Topps card in the 1987 Traded set when he played four years in the majors? He wasn't traded and he was definitely not a rookie.

Danny Jackson and Kevin McReynolds were two of a handful of young players in the mid-1980s who refused to sign individual contracts to appear on Topps cards, on the advice of the players' union. They apparently forced Topps to renegotiate with the union to obtain a blanket contract, covering all major leaguers.

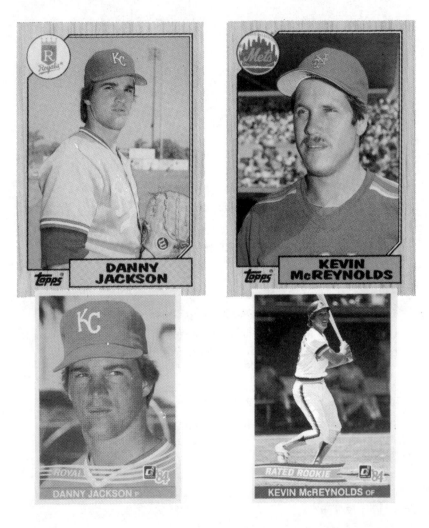

Why is Reggie Jackson in the 1988 Fleer and Score sets, but not in the Donruss or Topps sets?

The card companies were very much aware that the 1987 baseball season would be Jackson's last as an active player. Fleer and Score chose to include

Jackson as a tribute to his greatness. Donruss and Topps did not.

Why did Donruss make three Reggie Jackson cards in its 1981 set?

Probably to enhance the appeal of its set, Donruss issued more than one card of several superstars in its 1981 set.

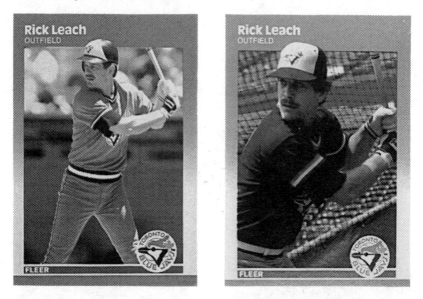

I have a question about the 1987 Fleer set and 1987 Fleer Update set. In the Fleer set, Rick Leach, #234, is featured with a Blue Jays uniform on. In the Fleer Update,

The Five Ws of Baseball Cards

Rick Leach, #63, is featured with the Blue Jays uniform again. Since he's not a rookie, and he didn't change teams since the two sets were made, why is he in the Update set?

The best possible explanation is Fleer did not know it had already shown Leach in the regular set, and issued an Update card.

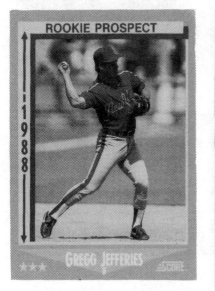 

Donruss, Fleer and Score included Gregg Jefferies in their 1988 sets. Why wasn't Jefferies in the 1988 Topps or Topps Traded sets?

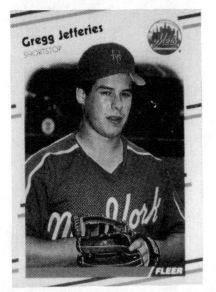 

In recent years, Topps has not included many rookies with little or no major league experience in its sets. That may be why Jefferies was not in the regular issue set put out by Topps in 1988. Topps probably withheld Jefferies from the 1988 Traded set so that his presence in the 1989 Topps set would be more meaningful. Perhaps Topps has changed its attitude toward rookies in its regular issue sets. Did you notice how many rookie cards can be found in the 1989 and 1990 Topps sets? There are many more than in previous years.

I'm working on my 1970 Topps set. I noticed on card #62, American League Batting Leaders, it states on the front that the leaders are Rod Carew, Reggie Smith and Tony Oliva. But on the back it lists Carew, Rich Reese of the Twins, and Oliva, with Smith fourth on the list. Why is this?

According to *The Baseball Encyclopedia,* Carew won the batting title that year with a .332 average, and Oliva and Smith tied for second with a .309 average. While Reese hit .322, he had only 419 at-bats, not quite enough to qualify him for the batting title.

In looking at the 1987 Donruss wax box, I noticed among the miniature reproductions of the cards in the set is a "Rated Rookie" card of some New York Yankee, mostly obscured by the Dale Murphy Diamond King card. The Rated Rookie does not appear in the Donruss set. Who is it? Why wasn't the card in the set?

There's no way to tell who the player is. This type of thing is common, since card boxes are usually designed and printed well in advance of the cards. There are similar cards on Topps boxes of the 1970s, and the 1984 Donruss wax box shows a Robin Yount card that differs from the issued version.

I have a question about Don Slaught. His 1984 and 1985 Topps cards say he's 6'0", 185 pounds, born 9-11-59. His 1987 Topps cards says he's 6'1", 190 pounds, born 9-11-58. His 1986 Topps cards says he's 6'0", 185 pounds, born 9-11-59. Which is right?

Well, they all are, sort of. It's not uncommon for teams — and players themselves — to fudge a little on heights, weights and ages, usually making a player taller, lighter and younger than he really is. For the record, the *Sporting News Official Baseball Register* says Slaught is 6'0", 185 pounds, born 10-11-59.

Don Mattingly's 1987 Topps card says his birth certificate shows he was born in 1962, not 1961, as has always been listed on his baseball cards and in publications.

The Five Ws of Baseball Cards

Why didn't he tell them his real birthdate, or was it an error in the publications and cards?

Young ball players frequently add a year or two to their age when they first turn pro to give them more "maturity" in the eyes of team officials. Later, they are likely to subtract a year or two to make them seem like a better long-range prospect.

I was looking at some 1958 Topps cards and noticed the Cleveland Indians logo shows the Indian wearing a crown. Why?

The crown was added to recognize the Indians' capture of the 1954 American League pennant. It was seen on Topps cards every year the company included team logos in the design — 1955, 1958, 1959, 1960 and 1965. When team logos returned in 1985, the crown was gone.

In the 1966 Topps set, the 7th Series checklist (#517) includes cards #507-598. All the price guides, however, indicate cards in the scarce high number series begin at #523. Why are cards 507-522 not considered in the high number series?

Topps' checklists of that era were not always exactly accurate in differentiating which cards were printed together. What Topps called a "series" back then may or may not have contained all of the cards printed together on one sheet. And since it is the quantity printed that generally determines value, collectors have learned to ignore Topps' definition of series. Specifically, since cards #507-522 were printed with the less-scarce "6th Series," and in greater quantity than cards #523-598, they are worth less today.

The 1981 Topps set contains only two American League outfielders with "All Star" across the top, Fred Lynn and Reggie Jackson. Is there another in the Traded set? Who?

There is not an "All Star" in the Traded set. The third outfielder for the 1980 A.L. All-Star team was Ben Oglivie. Topps just missed putting the banner on his card.

The 1982 Fleer rookie card of Jorge Bell shows him with Alan Ashby of the Houston Astros. What's going on here?

The picture was undoubtedly taken during spring training. Both the Blue Jays and Astros train in Florida.

Why is Mark Davidson in an outdated Twins uniform on his 1988 Topps card?

Because most photos used in a card set are taken during spring training the

The Five Ws of Baseball Cards

previous year and the teams usually wear their old style uniforms in spring training.

I bought four packs of 1989 Bowman cards. Three of the wrappers had different player designs on them. Why?

Just another throwback to the earlier Bowman issues, when several wrapper variations per year were common.

On the 1975 Topps card (#532) of Gorman Thomas, it shows him wearing #44. When Hank Aaron was on Milwaukee that year, his number was 44. So what's the deal?

Since many of the 1975 baseball card photos were taken at spring training the previous year, the Thomas photo shows him in the uniform he wore prior to Aaron joining the Brewers. Thomas surrendered #44 to the Hammer in 1975, switching to #3, then moving to #20 for the rest of his career.

On the 1987 Donruss card (#41) of Jerry Browne of the Rangers, he is wearing uniform #3, yet I was under the impression that his teammate Ruben Sierra wore that number.

Card #41 is indeed Jerry Browne. The photo was taken during spring training 1986 when Browne wore #3 and Sierra #47. Neither player started the 1986 season with the Rangers. Sierra was called up first and assigned #3; Browne arrived later and was assigned #8.

Blaine Beatty

The 1990 Upper Deck Blaine Beatty card #23 shows him wearing uniform #64 on the front, and #38 on the back. Is this an error card?

No. Many players, especially rookies, are photographed during spring training or during short call-ups to the big leagues wearing numbers other than those in which they later appear. Since card photos are often taken in spring training the previous year, it is not uncommon for a player to have changed uniform numbers.

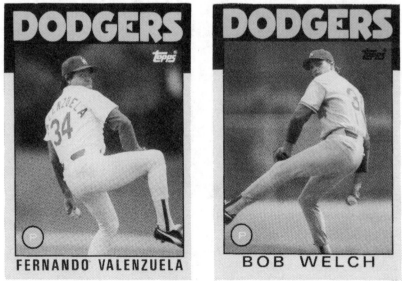

Why is Bob Welch wearing Fernando Valenzuela's uniform in the photo on his 1986 Topps card?

The background looks like this is a spring training photo. It could be Welch's own jerseys were in the wash or stolen. On close inspection, it looks like Topps' artists airbrushed off Valenzuela's name from the jersey, as well as a patch from the left sleeve.

My brother has a Classic 1990 Sammy Sosa card, #140. On the front it shows a Rangers player. On the back it shows he plays for the White Sox. The price guides don't list this as an error. Is it part of a traded set?

No. It's part of the regular 150-card issue. Sosa was traded from the Rangers to the White Sox on July 29, 1989, and Classic was unable to get a new photo of him in a White Sox uniform for the card. It has no effect on the card's value.

I have a 1990 Upper Deck card of Wade Boggs, #555. The back shows Bo Jackson and Boggs. What are they doing and where are they?

They are at home plate in Anaheim Stadium, where Boggs is congratulating Bo on his lead-off home run in the 1989 All-Star Game. Boggs was on deck at the time of the blast. The American League won, 5-3, and Bo was named MVP.

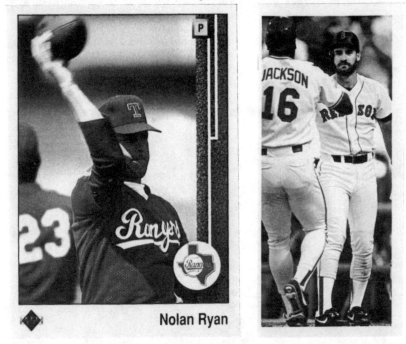

Nolan Ryan

I have a 1989 Upper Deck Nolan Ryan card (#774). Why is he throwing a football on the front of the card?

It's a conditioning exercise promoted by Texas Rangers pitching coach Tom House to help strengthen the arm by working out different muscles from those used in throwing a baseball. The exercise is gaining popularity among players, coaches and trainers.

I bought a collecting kit issued by Topps. The set contains a card of Dwight Gooden wearing #64. What's going on? He wears #16.

The photo was likely taken in spring training, 1984, or earlier. Before they make the team, rookies are usually given high uniform numbers because of the large number of players in training camp.

Why does the 1983 Topps John Denny card (#211) have a painted picture instead of a photograph?

It's not exactly painted, although there is some paint there. What was originally a picture of Denny in a Cleveland Indians uniform has been airbrushed to make him a Philadelphia Phillie. Airbrushing is not uncommon. Topps has been airbrushing for years.

On the "Home Plate Heroes" card of Eric Davis that appeared on Kraft Macaroni and Cheese boxes, he's resting a bat on his right shoulder. All that's showing is the handle. Where's the rest of the bat?

It appears to have been lost in the airbrushing done to remove the Reds logo from the batting helmet and to improve the color of the background sky.

The bottom of the bat knob pictured on Gregg Jefferies' 1990 Upper Deck card says "MAZ." What does that mean?

It means when the photographer came around, Jefferies grabbed a bat owned by then-teammate Lee Mazzilli.

127

The Five Ws of Baseball Cards

Why was Tom Seaver's uniform airbrushed on the 1986 Topps Traded card?

Because Topps didn't have enough time to get a real photo of Seaver in his Red Sox uniform after he was traded from the White Sox on June 29 that year.

On the 1980 Topps Padres Future Stars card (#685), why does it appear that Tim Flannery is a painting and the other two players are photographs?

Because the Flannery photo has been heavily retouched by an airbrush artist. It looks as if a minor league black-and-white photo was painted over in color to make Flannery appear in a San Diego uniform.

Why is Mike Laga's jersey on his 1987 Topps card (#321) in flourescent pink?

Because Topps' airbrush artist evidently didn't know what color a Cardinals uniform was when he painted over Laga's Tigers uniform.

Some of my Donruss sets have loose cards, while other sets are wrapped in cellophane. Why the difference?

The cards wrapped in cellophane are sorted and packaged by Donruss, and known in the hobby as "factory" sets. The loose cards are generally made and packaged by dealers out of wax packs, etc. In all years, the Donruss factory sets contain corrected versions of error cards produced in the earlier wax- and rack-pack issues, and are usually considered to be worth more money.

Is there a reason why Mark Grace and Chris Sabo always come in 1989 Topps packs together. I get wax, cello, rack ... any kind of packs and they are always together.

It's called "collation." The way Topps cuts and packs its cards, the same cards show up together time and time again. When you learn the sequence for each year, you can cherry-pick stars and hot rookies among rack and cello packs.

As do many other collectors, I like to receive the finest quality grade of card when ordering by mail. So, what is the difference between a factory set and a Mint set of cards?

A factory set is collated (put together) and packaged by the card manufacturer, by machine. Because the human element is eliminated, such sets may have cards which are poorly printed, off-center, or otherwise flawed. If you buy a set described as Mint, you should get a set that has been assembled by hand, with every card inspected for problems. If you get a damaged card in a factory set, it's unlikely you'll get a replacement. If you buy a Mint set that has flawed cards, the seller should be willing to exchange them for true Mint cards.

In a 1988 Topps wax pack, I received two each of Chris James, Todd Worrell, Fred Manrique and Bob Forsch. They were all back-to-back in the pack. How would this happen? Are cards put in the pack by machine or hand?

It's a good question that can't be answered because Topps won't release information of that nature. We do know that cards are inserted in the packs by machine. Similar sequences of card numbers appear in wax, cello and rack packs, but what you discovered was very unusual. It sounds like a production screw-up by Topps. This type of poor decollation has been going on since card companies started putting more than one card in a pack.

I opened a 1989 Donruss rack pack and got the best pack I ever got. Included were Jose Canseco, Don Mattingly, Eric Davis, Wade Boggs, Tim Raines, Cal Ripken, Mike Scott, Wally Joyner and Gary Carter. Do you think there was a mistake in the way it was packaged? Is there a constant pattern on what cards are found together in a pack?

Topps packs (wax, rack and cello) adhere to a regular pattern in most instances. However, in the past, that has not been the case with Donruss. You just got very lucky.

My friend recently opened a box of 1989 Donruss wax packs. In the box were 14 Ken Hills, 12 Dennis Rasmussens, 10 Ron Oesters and three other players with eight cards each. Is this possible or has this box been tampered with?

This type of duplication is quite common in recent Donruss wax boxes. Look at the bright side: it's also possible to find boxes with a dozen Ken Griffey Jr. cards.

Has anyone noticed a scarcity of 1989 Upper Deck cards in the 400 numbers? I have purchased about 1,000 cards at different places and only 40 of the 1,000 are 400 numbers. Did I have bad luck or are these cards scarce?

The mix of 1989 Upper Deck in early packs, boxes and cases was not good. This type of shortage is reported all over the country, although others who report the problem find other numbers to be in short supply. It looks like it will even out in the end, and encourage some trading in the meantime.

I received a 1988 Donruss Baseball's Best set for a gift. In looking through them, I noticed I was missing card #12. Am I unlucky or is it normal for some sets to be missing cards? Could you tell me where I could get another card #12 to complete my set? Maybe I could write Donruss.

Because the cutting and packaging of baseball cards is a mechanical operation, it is very possible to find a set short of one or more cards (or with extra cards, for that matter). Assuming the set you received was still factory sealed, you'll have to chalk the loss up to bad luck and try to find the card you need at your next card show.

Many dealers at shows break up sets like this to sell as singles. In most cases, buying a replacement will be easier, cheaper and quicker than writing to the card companies — most of which totally ignore such requests. If you buy a hand-collated set from a dealer, however, you have the right to expect him to make good on any missing cards.

I purchased a Will Clark Burger King 2nd-Edition All-Pro Series card. It has his biography and all his 1986 statistics. The card was approved by the Major League Baseball Players Association. If that's the case, why isn't there a logo on his hat?

For team logos to appear on baseball cards, they have to be sanctioned by Major League Baseball. The MLBPA approval is needed to get the player on the cards; MLB approval is needed to get the logo on the card. If a card isn't approved by both organizations and shows players and team logos, it's probably an unauthorized issue. All the major sets have the approval of both organizations.

How come all of the 1989 Cap'n Crunch cereal cards are missing team logos on their caps? Was this done on purpose? If so, what is the point?

It was done on purpose. The point is to avoid having to pay a royalty to the teams for the depiction of their insignias.

I know most of the stipulations to Pete Rose's banishment from baseball, but I do have one question. Is it possible for a major card company to make a card of Rose in uniform, such as a tribute card, record-holder card, flashback card, etc., since it is licensed by Major League Baseball and the Major League Baseball Players Association?

While the baseball establishment cannot officially prohibit the card companies from doing what you suggest, it is unlikely any of them would be willing to jeopardize their license status by putting Pete Rose on a new issue.

I am a baseball card collector who is also an amateur photographer. Who takes the pictures for the card companies? Are they staff photographers or are they sports photographers for newspapers and magazines who take the card pictures on the side? How could I get involved in taking pictures for card companies?

Generally, the card companies acquire their photos from a small group of free-lance photographers who specialize in the genre. Many of the photographers also shoot for the magazines, including *Sports Collectors Digest* and *Baseball Cards* magazine.

It is very difficult for an amateur to break in. The companies prefer to deal with a handful of photographers who can supply hundreds of images, rather than hundreds of photographers. If you want to buck long odds, send an inquiry with a few sample photos — samples you won't miss if they are not returned — to the art director of the card company.

Factors Relating to Card Values

Chapter Five

What's the difference in values between a regular Donruss set and a Donruss-Leaf, and Topps and O-Pee-Chee?

Although there are fewer Leaf (Canadian versions of Donruss cards) sets made than the corresponding Donruss version, there is nowhere near the demand for them, so they are priced about the same. The same is true for Topps and O-Pee-Chee cards, although some of the older O-Pee-Chee stars and rookie cards are priced lower than their Topps counterparts.

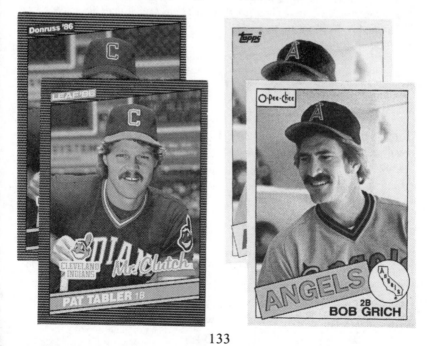

Factors Relating to Card Values

Why is it every time I get a baseball card price guide there is no O-Pee-Chee in it? Is this because they are not worth anything or is it just because you don't want to be bothered printing the prices for it?

We suspect the price guides you get are all published in the United States. Collectors on this side of the border have little or no interest in OPC cards, so printing values for them would be an inefficient use of space. There are several Canadian card publications now; they should have the information you seek.

Regarding value, are factory sets better than hand-sorted sets? What about vending sets?

In recent years, factory sets have sometimes contained scarcer and higher-priced variation cards that were not available in card packs. Hand-sorted (or hand-collated) sets will almost always contain the cheapest variations in a set. A vending set (assembled from vending boxes) will be free of gum and wax stains. All things considered, factory sets (especially factory-sealed sets) have proven to be the most valuable of the sets.

At a show, I noticed that Topps factory sets were being sold at a higher price than the hand-collated sets. The factory sets were not sealed and simply had the Topps name printed on an otherwise plain box. Does hand-collation reduce the value of a complete set? Do the boxes actually come from Topps, or are they handmade?

The complete sets which dealers can order directly from Topps come in the boxes you described. In dealing strictly with Topps sets, it does not make sense for a hand-collated set to be worth less (assuming both sets contain the exact same versions of cards).

Theoretically, at least, the person putting together the hand-collated set would have screened it for badly miscut, creased or otherwise damaged cards. That is not necessarily the case with a factory-packaged set.

I bought a 1989 Donruss factory set. When I opened the set, I saw the cards were neatly grouped and wrapped in plastic. Will it devaluate the set if I remove the plastic?

Yes. Donruss factory sets with the cards unwrapped bring less money than those that have not been opened.

I purchased a 1989 Fleer factory set at a card shop. The dealer said he didn't know which variation of the Billy Ripken card was in the set. If I were to break the factory seal to look at the Ripken card, is the set still a "factory" set?

Sure, but it won't be worth as much as a set with the seal intact. Like it or not, cards are more valuable if they are untouched by human hands.

Are there any reprint sets worth buying? I have never read anything good about them.

The only reprint sets worth buying are those that you will personally enjoy. Except for the "official" 1952 Topps reprint (currently selling for around $200), they will never have any collector value because they can always be reprinted when demand increases.

Does the sponsor's name on the bottom of a police card change its value? My local department had 500 sets printed with "Mauston P.D." on the bottom; the Wisconsin State Patrol had 5,000 sets.

There are only a handful of people who are attempting to collect all department variations of the police sets. Generally, most collectors are happy with a single set, regardless of the issuing department. In Wisconsin, more than 50 police departments sponsor the Brewers police set each year.

I have a complete 1982 Topps set that has a price guide value of $100. However, the total value of all 792 singles exceeds $200. Why is this?

With older sets (pre-1974), the complete set price is usually equal to or greater than the sum total of the individual cards. Dealers normally place a premium on a complete set because of the amount of effort expended in putting it together.

This isn't the case with recent sets. Most dealers who sell recent complete sets are selling the factory-collated sets. No work is involved in making these sets, so no premium is attached. And because collectors/investors have taken to hoarding large groups of certain players in recent sets, dealers can make more money selling singles or lots rather than complete sets.

Factors Relating to Card Values

How do you price baseball cards? Do you take a survey?

We employ the hobby's only full-time price guide analyst to set the card values that appear in our magazines. We rely on input from a panel of selected dealers and collectors around the country, as well as our observations of card prices in mail order ads, at card shops, at card shows and off a nationwide dealer teletype wire. We prefer to key our listings to actual sales prices. Too often surveys reflect prices that the person being surveyed wishes a card to be, rather than the reality of the marketplace.

Why is the 1981 Drake's "Big Hitter" set the least expensive of all Drake's sets? I thought that consistently in the baseball card hobby that the first of anything is the most valuable.

Usually, but not always. In the case of Drake's the company dumped tons of the 1981 set into the hobby market late in the season. The set, which collectors had been led to believe would be available only by buying boxes of snack cakes, was once selling for more than $15, but dropped to way under $5 after they came onto the market in quantity. Having learned a lesson, Drake's produced fewer in subsequent years. Thus, it's simply a case of the oldest (1981) issue being more plentiful than the newer versions.

Why hasn't the 1983 Donruss Hall of Fame Heroes set attained much value?

Mostly because collectors aren't very enthusiastic about sets of non-current players. Also, the artwork on the cards was not popular with collectors.

Why are Topps "Tiffany" sets worth so much?

The limited-edition "Tiffany" sets sell at a sharply higher price than their corresponding regular Topps sets because there are fewer of them on the market. For example, there were 10,000 Tiffany sets produced in 1984, and 5,000 in 1985 and 1986. Compare those numbers with the hundreds of thousands of regular issue sets.

I would like to know how much more a Tiffany glossy card is worth compared to a regular card.

There is no set formula. You can get an idea by comparing the prices of glossy sets versus regular sets. A 1985 Topps Tiffany set, for example, sells for about $600, while the "regular" set brings $110. More recent Topps Tiffany sets sell for $100 to $125 each, compared to $25 to $30 for the regular versions.

I've been collecting Topps Tiffany sets since they began in 1984. I have often wanted to look at them, but the factory put a gold seal on the box. Would breaking it reduce the value of the set?

Breaking the seal should theoretically not reduce the resale value of the set, but it may make it harder to sell. A potential buyer might want to go through the set card by card to examine the condition and make sure all the key players are there before buying.

Why are the 1984-1986 Donruss baseball card sets so drastically different in price from the 1981-1983 sets?

Differences in printed quantities account for the price difference. After three years of overproduction, Donruss drastically cut back in 1984, to more closely meet true demand. When collecting boomed, demand exceeded supply and prices climbed.

I bought the 1985 Fleer Update set and it came in a faded box. Does the value decrease?

Generally, anytime you do anything to alter a baseball card item from the way it was originally issued you decrease the value. Yes, a beat-up box does decrease the value of a compete set of Traded or Update cards since it is part of the "original issue" package.

I have a 1986 Fleer "Baseball's Best" set. It has six team stickers included. Are the stickers considered part of the set? If you don't have them, does that decrease the value of the set?

For the many specialty sets which have proliferated since 1981, the appropriate box, stickers, puzzles and other insert items which were part of the original packaging should be considered as needed to have a truly "complete" set.

I purchased the full set of 1988 Score cards. Since this is the first year of Score cards, do you think in the years to come it would be worth as much as the 1952 Topps set is now?

Hardly. The 1952 Topps set is worth $50,000 because so few are available. It's a safe bet there are fewer than 100 Near Mint 1952 Topps sets around. It's also a safe bet that there are a couple of hundred thousand of 1988 Score sets in collector hands.

Which of the 1987 sets, Donruss or Fleer, do you think will end up with a higher value?

Our personal opinion — Donruss. It's not as readily available today, and has the edge in numbers of quality rookie cards.

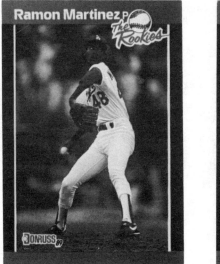

Why is the 1989 Donruss "The Rookies" set so scarce and expensive?

Dealer allocations on this issue were very small, leading hobbyists to believe the entire set was printed in relatively short supply. With a lot of hot rookies in the set, its value took off immediately.

Factors Relating to Card Values

Will the value of the small boxed card sets from stores such as K-Mart, Kay Bee and Circle K ever increase?

We happen to like these boxed sets because they contain many superstar singles. If you don't pay too much for these oddball cards/sets, they should prove to be very profitable in the long run. There are millions of cards made by each of the major companies in their annual sets, while production of the small sets can be measured in the tens of thousands. We believe in coming years these sets will be in great demand.

Single Card Values

Do you think one day Cal Ripken, Dale Murphy or Mike Schmidt cards may be as valuable as Mickey Mantle cards are today?

140

In general, no. Mantle cards are valuable because only a few thousand of each survived to try to satisfy demand from hundreds of thousands of collectors. Cards of today's top stars were generally printed in number of a half a million or more, with a larger percentage still in collectors hands. The ratio of cards to collector seems to be too high to expect prices of recent cards to reach levels similar to Mantle. Remember that Mantle is generally acknowledged as the all-time favorite ballplayer among collectors.

The 1951 Bowman Mickey Mantle is priced at $5,000, while his 1952 Topps is at $20,000. Shouldn't his rookie card be worth more than his second-year card?

Not necessarily. All card values depend on supply and demand. In this case, even though 1951 Bowman Mantles are even more scarce than 1952 Topps Mantles, there is enough greater demand for the Topps card to cause its price to be greater than the Bowman card. There have always been more collectors of Topps cards than of Bowman, thus the price difference.

Why are the cards of players such as Ozzie Smith and Jeff Reardon priced so low?

Defensive standouts and pitchers (especially relief pitchers) receive less collector interest than do home run hitters or batting champs.

I wondered why the 1952 Topps card #1, Andy Pafko, is worth so much.

The 1952 Pafko card is worth so much in high grades — $1,200 in Near Mint — because it's the first card in the set, and the most susceptible to damage.

Factors Relating to Card Values

Think about it: kids back then, like kids today, carried their cards everywhere — in numerical order. The top card caught the brunt of the scuffs and dings and dents. Also, cards were often held together by a rubber band. The card that bore the brunt of that abuse was, again, the first card. So truly top-grade Pafko cards are very, very hard to locate, and demand a high price. Lower grade Pafkos bring only a common price.

I traded my 1951 Topps Red Back Monte Irvin rookie. Why is this card worth less than his 1954 Topps card? Why is this Hall of famer's rookie card worth so little?

The answer is the same to both questions. The 1951 Topps sets (both red backs and blue backs) are not popular with collectors. It takes demand to make cards valuable.

I have a 1955 Topps Karl Spooner rookie card (#90). It shows in 1954 he won two complete games, gave up seven hits, no runs and struck out 27, with six walks and a cool 0.00 ERA. Why is this card considered only a common?

A phenomenal rookie season does not make a player a star. Spooner pitched in only 29 more games in his major league career — all in 1955. A sore arm ended his career following the World Series in 1955. Lifetime, his 10-6 record, 3.09 ERA and 105 strikeouts don't qualify this "one-year wonder" for star status.

The picture on Steve Carlton's rookie card is airbrushed to show him in the uniform of the Cardinals. Does this decrease the value of the card?

The airbrushing, while it may make the card less visually appealing, really has no material effect on its value.

142

I got a Rickey Henderson/Lou Brock card in an Upper Deck low number box. I then bought a high number box and got the same card, except the date "May 1, 1991" is printed above the number 939 on the base. This is missing on the low series card. Which card is rarer and more valuable?

Neither is rare, but the dated version is scarcer. Whether it will attain any significant premium value will be determined by collector demand — we don't anticipate that happening.

Enclosed is a copy of a 1990 Upper Deck card I found in a pack I opened. My checklist says card #702 should be the Expos "Rookie Threats" card, but mine is Mike Witt. There is a big black box on the back that obscures most of the picture and stats. None of the dealers by me know anything about it. Maybe you do?

You've found a very rare card. Mike Witt, who went to the Yankees from the Angels early in the 1990 season, was bumped from the Upper Deck high number set by the popular Expos rookie card. Only a few Witt cards were ever printed, and as indicated by the overprinted box on the back of the card, they were supposed to have been destroyed rather than issued. Fewer than 50 of these are in known collector hands. The card has been selling for $200.

I have heard so much about the 1977 Burger King Lou Piniella card. Why is the card priced at $25?

It was printed in much shorter supply than the other 1977 Burger King Yankees. Sparky Lyle in his book, *"The Bronx Zoo,"* says Piniella complained to Yankee boss George Steinbrenner when his card wasn't included in the original set, and that Steinbrenner pressured Burger King into adding a Piniella card to the set.

I have a black-and-white 1982 Oneonta Yankees card of John Elway. An annual price guide book says the entire set is $130. I know that minor league sets do not sell well, but could you give me an idea of how much the Elway card is worth?

Assuming it's genuine (black-and-white minor league cards are easy to counterfeit; that's why they're usually bought and sold in sets), since the Elway card is the only one in the set which isn't a common, it would be worth at least $125 of the $130 set price.

143

Factors Relating to Card Values

I have a 1982 TCMA Tidewater Tides card of Darryl Strawberry which has nothing printed on the back. Is it valuable or scarce?

It's somewhat scarce, but not as valuable as the "real" Strawberry minor league card. This was printed long after 1982 as a "promotional" item. Since it was not issued with the rest of the Tidewater set in 1982, most collectors don't consider it to be legitimate.

Why is the 1984 Mike Schmidt Donruss card more valuable than the 1981, 1982 or 1983 Donruss cards? Usually it is the older cards that are worth more.

Older cards are usually worth more because there were fewer of them printed. The exact opposite is true in the case of 1981-1984 Donruss. There were fewer 1984 Donruss printed than in 1981, 1982 or 1983, so when demand heats up, the value rises quickly for the 1984 cards.

I was lucky enough to find a 1984 Topps card of Don Mattingly by looking through rack packs. Tell me why a 1984 Donruss Mattingly is worth $80 and a 1984 Topps Mattingly is only worth $25?

The difference in values is that there are fewer 1984 Donruss cards than 1984 Topps cards.

I have a 1985 Topps "Super" 5" by 7" card of Dwight Gooden. Is it worth as much as his regular 1985 Topps rookie card?

Surprisingly, no. You'd think it would be since the "Super" card is many times rarer than the regular 1985 Topps Gooden cards. But because a large number of

144

collectors don't buy anything that isn't 2½" by 3½", the larger Gooden card sells for around $2, while the regular card is at $9.

I have a 1986 Fleer League Leader card of Jose Canseco. This is his rookie card. How come it is only worth $3.50?

Because it is not his "real" rookie card. By definition, a rookie card has to be part of the regularly-issued annual set by one of the major card companies. Regionals, boxed sets, Traded and Update sets don't qualify for true rookie card status.

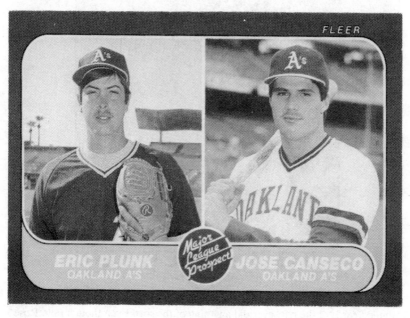

I was wondering why the 1986 Jose Canseco cards range so widely in price. The Topps Traded is $9, the Major League Prospect card from Fleer is $50, and the Donruss Rated Rookie is $90.

Supply and demand. While the 1986 Topps Traded is actually numerically scarcer than the Fleer or Donruss cards, not as many people want it because a Traded or Update card isn't considered a "real" rookie card. The difference in price between the Fleer and Donruss is attributable to the fact that the Donruss card is somewhat scarcer, but pictures Canseco alone, while the Fleer card is shared with Eric Plunk.

In looking at Eric Davis material, I've come across what could be an interesting card in the future. It is Tony Perez' Topps 1986 card, #85, which shows Perez being congratulated at home plate by Davis. This would make the card a must in the future for Davis fans. Do you think Davis' appearance on the Perez card will increase the value?

No, because there is no evidence that the presence of superstars on other common cards of the past ever did anything of the sort. Even though Pete Rose appears as a base runner on Chris Short's 1971 Topps card, #511, it commands no premium value.

I traded a 1986 Donruss Rated Rookie card of Jose Canseco in Very Good condition for 1977 rookie cards of Jack Clark and Andre Dawson. Both cards were Near Mint. Was this a good deal?

For you it was. Cards of the 1980s in Very Good condition have almost no collector appeal, since there are hundreds of thousands of them available in Near Mint or better.

Will the baseball cards that go with the Starting Lineup figurines ever be worth anything?

We'd guess they'll be worth about the same or a little more than the regular cards from the major companies of the corresponding year.

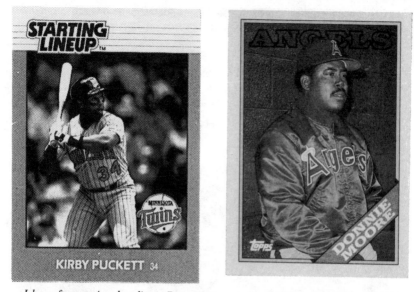

I have former Angels reliever Donnie Moore's latest Topps card from 1988. In 1989, he killed himself after being released from the minor leagues. Does the future look good for his cards?

No. His cards were commons when he was alive and he's not going to be improving his career stats now. The fact that he died infamously won't add any value to them.

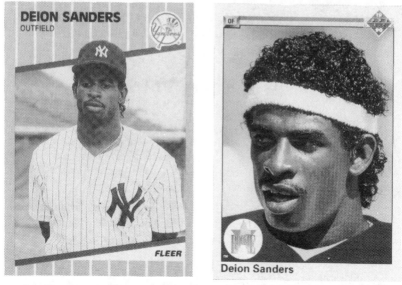

If Deion Sanders doesn't play baseball again and becomes a successful football player, do you think his 1989 update cards will go up like John Elways's minor league baseball cards?

No, because there are tens of thousands of updates made by each company, and Elway's minor league card was probably in a quantity of just a couple of thousand.

Why is the 1990 Score Bo Jackson football/baseball black-and-white card worth $4? It is a card that should not even be in the set.

Most collectors disagree with your assessment of the appropriateness of this card in the 1990 Score set. That's why it's $4; simple supply and demand.

Uncut Sheet Values

During a recent remodeling job in my home, I discovered some 1964-1968 Topps uncut sheets. Although the outer cards are in poor condition, the cards in the center are fine. Would it be wise to have the sheets professionally cut or leave them as they are? I also found a roll of 1966 Topps wrappers. Do these have any value? I'd like to sell these items. Where would I get the best price for them?

Leave the sheets as they are. To get top dollar for them, place an ad in *Sports Collectors Digest* and auction them off to the highest bidder. Nice condition wrappers from 1966 sell for $10-$15 each.

I traded for an uncut sheet of 30 identical Roberto Clemente Fan Club cards issued by the Daily Juice Co., Oakmont, Pa. Do they have any premium value?

Issued in about 1970, these fan-club cards are still relatively plentiful in hobby channels. We've seen them sell for $2 apiece at shows, and they are quite often found as uncut sheets.

In 1971, I was a consolation prize winner in a Topps contest. I won an uncut sheet of 1971 cards. They are in no particular numerical order and each card is duplicated on the sheet. Stars are Reggie Jackson, Phil Niekro, Pete Rose, Bert Blyleven, Bill Mazeroski and Thurman Munson. It's still in the original box with the postmark. I wrote to Topps to ask about them, but they just sent a form letter with dealers' addresses. Were these available to the public or just to prize winners? How many were issued? How valuable is it?

Since these are rarely encountered, it has to be assumed they were not available to the public. If Topps can't tell you how many were made, we certainly can't, although you'd have to figure that their status as a consolation prize would mean several hundred or several thousand were made. We'd estimate value at two or three times the total value of the cards.

My son bought a grab bag at a show that contained an uncut sheet of 1981 Batting and Pitching Leaders cards, with two players for each team, such as Houston's

149

Art Howe and Nolan Ryan. Is this sheet worth anything?

Nothing more than the value of the individual cards. This sounds like part of a regular 1982 Topps 132-card uncut sheet that somebody dismembered to get the good cards. The team leader cards have little value.

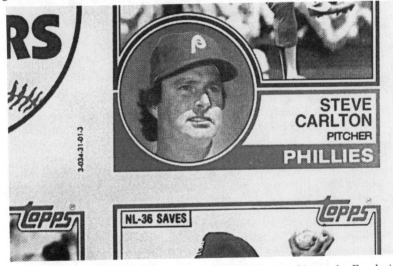

The 1983 Topps wax packs had a contest card that you could scratch off and win prizes. I won an uncut sheet of nine 1982 league leaders cards. They are mostly like the regular 1983 Topps cards of the same players, but they have a blank back and in the corner is a panel giving the category in which the player led his league. Does this uncut panel have any real value?

Not much. Some dealers acquired large numbers of the sheets and they can still be bought at shows for $1 or $2 each.

I have a 1983 Topps Wade Boggs rookie on an uncut panel with three common players. The two top cards have a significant crease. How much is the value of the Boggs card affected by being on an uncut sheet? How do the creased cards affect the price?

Because the 1983 Topps cards were rather widely available in full 132-card uncut sheets, and because it is very hard to store, display or ship such sheets, the presence of a Boggs rookie card on a full sheet would add little or no premium value. Your four-card panel was evidently cut off such a sheet. As such it has absolutely no premium value, considering the crease.

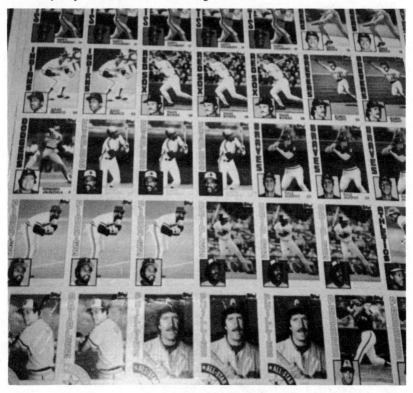

I recently bought an uncut sheet of 1984 Topps cards. It has stars such as Don Mattingly, Mike Schmidt, Wade Boggs and Darryl Strawberry. Unfortunately, the Schmidt card has a large crease. My friend says it is not worth anything. Is that true?

Your friend is wrong. Although a heavily-creased 1984 Schmidt card is worthless, the rest of the cards on the sheet hold their value. You could, for instance, cut out the Mattingly, Strawberry and other star cards and, if cut properly, they would be worth current value. The sheet itself is also worth a small premium, even with a few creased cards.

151

Factors Relating to Card Values

I acquired two uncut sheets of the 1984 Nestle cards produced by Topps. The sheets contain the cards of Don Mattingly, Wade Boggs, Darryl Strawberry and other stars. Dealers I've talked with are reluctant to give me an idea as to the value of the sheets. Can you help?

Several dealers have had the six sheets that make up the complete set of 792 cards professionally cut into individual cards. A reported 4,000 sets were produced by Topps, and we've seen complete sets being offered for more than $475. The Mattingly rookie card usually has an asking price of $275.

When cut well, single cut-up cards are more valuable than a set of uncut sheets, unlike most other uncut sheets. If you decide to have the sheets cut up, have them done professionally, because poorly cut cards will have little or no value.

I own a 1985 Topps uncut sheet that contains the rookie cards of Eric Davis and Roger Clemens. Should I keep the cards in sheet form or have them professionally cut into single cards?

We suggest keeping the sheet intact. We believe it will have greater value in years to come.

I received an uncut sheet of 20 Jiffy Pop popcorn cards. Do cards like this ever become valuable?

Sure. In fact, the 1986-1988 Jiffy Pop sets are some of the scarest give-away cards of the late 1980s. Like any card, their future will depend on supply and demand within the hobby.

Are the cards on the Topps wax boxes worth less if they are cut from the box?

Complete boxes have greater value, but it is much easier to display the cards by cutting them from the box.

153

Unopened Pack Values

I have an unopened pack of 1980 Topps baseball cards made to be sold with Squirt soda. There is a Squirt advertising card and three regular Topps cards of that year in a cellophane package. I have a pack with Rickey Henderson's rookie card on top. Is this item rare? How were they distributed?

We'd rate your pack quite highly, on the basis that these Squirt packs are seldom found anywhere, and one with Henderson on top would be in especially strong demand. The packs were intended to be given away with purchases of a carton of soda. The next year, the company issued two-card panels that hung directly on the soda bottles.

Why are rack packs and cellos worth more with the star on the top than on the bottom. It's the same card, isn't it?

Yes, the card is the same, but racks and cellos with stars showing are not bought for the cards themselves, but rather as a display piece, and for the relative scarcity of the item. Since the front of the card is more important than the back, packs with stars showing on front command a higher premium. As a rule of thumb, figure the star on top to be worth about 50 percent more than the same pack with the star on bottom.

I have a 1988 Mark Grace rookie card showing on a Donruss rack pack. Is it worth it to keep it sealed or should I open it?

Collectors of star-showing rack and cello packs will pay a significant premium for a 1988 Donruss rack with Grace showing on top. A general rule of thumb in judging the value of such items is to multiply the value of the card two to three times. If, at a later date, you want to sell and can't find a buyer at that premium value, you can always open the rack and sell the card on its own merits.

I picked up a 1989 Topps cello pack with Mark Grace on the bottom. How much is this pack worth? Also, how much would a cello with Grace on front be worth?

A 1989 Topps Grace goes for around $1.00. With Grace on the bottom, the pack is worth around $2-$3; with Grace on top, about $ 3.50-$5.

I realize packs with stars showing on top or bottom bring a higher price. I have some 1989 Score packs where you can see who is on top or bottom. Would these have any higher value since it is difficult to see who the player is without looking closely?

As a rule of thumb, the harder it is to see the star card in an unopened pack, the lower the premium over the card's single value.

Why do 1991 Upper Deck packs cost so much more than other packs?

Because of the high quality of the cards, they cost more to make. Also, collector demand is higher for Upper Deck than for most other brands.

I have many premium cards which are laminated with a plastic called U-Seal-It. Most of the cards are Mint, and the lamination has not faded or caused any visual damage. How does this influence the grade and value of my cards?

It virtually destroys the value. The cards may look Mint now, but any attempt to remove the lamination will wreck them completely. It's unlikely a buyer would pay more than Poor price for laminated cards.

Miscellaneous Items

Do you think Donruss Diamond King puzzles will ever be worth anything?

No.

Are team logo stickers in the Fleer packs worth anything?

They're worth collecting as an adjunct to a complete set, but they currently have no monetary value.

I bought some Leaf wax boxes from a dealer that have not Leaf but regular Donruss cards in the packs. The packs don't appear to have been tampered with; they

Factors Relating to Card Values

seem a legitimate oddity. Is there extra value to these miswrapped packs?

No. Because most wax packs can be very easily tampered with, there is no extra value to miswraps. If they were valuable, it would be too easy to fake. Many Topps cards from the 1950s through the 1970s can be found in wrappers (and boxes) of the wrong year.

*Do the cards given away in **Baseball Cards** magazine and **Sports Illustrated for Kids** have any value?*

Their values are determined the same way as any other baseball card — supply and demand. We have not seen any great demand for the cards as singles, but back copies of the magazines containing the cards sell for as much as $20 on the aftermarket. We do not offer a back-issue service.

I just bought 30 of the 1981 Topps Scratch-Off cards. Are they valuable?

The scratch-offs have very little value.

I purchased a 1983 Fleer sticker panel with Wade Boggs on it. Since it's his rookie year, shouldn't it be priced higher than 75 cents?

Like most of the 1980s stickers, stamps and other subsidiary sets, they were not very popular when issued, and, although they are relatively hard to find, are not expensive today.

I have a box of 1985 Topps wax packs that do not have the All-Star Game trip promotion on the front. Is this scarce? Are they worth keeping unopened?

While undated 1985 Topps packs are considerably scarcer than the dated version, there is little collector demand for the recent wrapper variations. Thus, it is unlikely that they will ever be worth a significant premium on that account. Most dealers charge about twice as much for the undated variety.

Do the special offer cards, such as the "Spring Fever" contest cards in the 1987 Topps packs, have any premium value?

Not yet, but they may in the future. Since many collectors send these cards in to order the special glossy sets, and most others throw them away, they could be scarce some day. Some of the contest and premium cards issued in Topps packs in the late 1950s sell for up to $20 today.

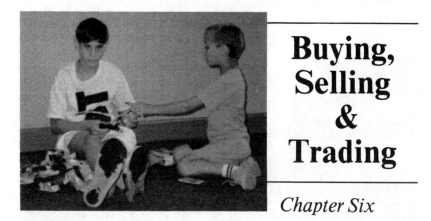

Buying, Selling & Trading

Chapter Six

What is the best place to buy, sell and trade baseball cards? A show? A shop? Or through the mail?

All three places have their advantages.

Shows — Shows offer a great number of sellers who have a great amount of material. Many a checklist has been filled by spending an afternoon at a card show. Also, the number of dealers breeds competition. You can browse from table to table to find the best deal, and, if selling or trading cards, you can go from dealer to dealer to get the best offer. Another advantage of shows is they often feature a current or former major leaguer available to sign autographs. Most of the time, there is a fee for the autograph.

Shops — The main attraction of a baseball card shop or store is the time you have available to look over the owner's items. Also, you can ask the dealer to be on the look out for certain things you collect, perhaps obscure or hard-to-locate items. And repeat business at a store can lead to some discounts or good deals for your repeat business.

Magazines or other periodicals — The main benefit of conducting business through hobby magazines such as *Sports Collectors Digest, Card News, Sports Card Price Guide Monthly* and *Baseball Cards* is the sheer volume of advertisers and the most varied card and memorabilia selection anywhere. Whether it's a T-206 Honus Wagner or a game-worn Don Mattingly uniform, these magazines will have it.

If I was to sell my baseball cards to a dealer, how much would he give me?

When selling to a dealer, expect to be offered as little as 10 percent of the price guide value for common cards, and from 50 to 80 percent of the price guide for stars and rookies. (These are approximate figures — every transaction is different.) The faster a dealer can sell a particular item has a lot to do with how much he will pay for it. The same is true with sets. If you have a set valued at $100 and the dealer knows he can sell quickly, he'll probably offer you $70-$80 for it. But if it's a set that isn't selling well, expect from $50-$60. Trading with a dealer is similar. A dealer works on a profit margin, and he would be out of business in no time if he were to trade $1 in merchandise for $1 in merchandise.

If you have the time and energy, you may want to try to retail the cards yourself, by setting up a table at a show, or by placing an ad in one of the publications listed in this book. Some dealers will take cards on consignment. And telephone auctions are good places to sell your cards. Auctions, like consignments, will charge a fee for selling your cards, usually between 5 and 20 percent.

I haven't been collecting baseball cards for too long. What would be more valuable? Selling the complete set of cards, or selling the cards from the set individually?

For recent sets, the value of the individual cards is much greater than the cost of the complete set. For sets produced before 1974, the complete set price is the same or greater than the sum of the individual cards.

Aren't I taking my chances ordering cards through the mail? Couldn't the dealer just take my money and not deliver the cards?

Sure, it could happen, but it very rarely does. Such "dealers" don't last long in the hobby anyway. Word travels fast about such rip-off artists. Rest assured, there aren't many bad apples to begin with.

Krause Publications, the publisher of the magazines mentioned in one of the previous answers, screens all of its display advertisers through a reference check of their hobby contacts. Also, advertisers who demonstrate an inability to provide customers with an acceptable level of customer service are banned from advertising in any Krause magazine. This has been done to ensure collectors can buy from, sell to and trade with these advertisers with complete confidence.

If you're a beginning collector (or any collector for that matter), find a dealer or dealers you're comfortable doing business with, and continue doing business with them. You can just as easily build a rapport with a mail order dealer as you can with your local hobby store dealer, and reap the benefits of that relationship. To find those dealers, we suggest you place a small order with them and see if they deliver your merchandise promptly, safely and in the condition they advertised. If the dealer was courteous and fair with a "small" order, the chances are good he'll be the same with a bigger order.

Please tell me the best way not to get taken when selling my cards by mail when answering the classified ads in your publications.

The best way is to deal with persons who advertise there each issue for a long period of time. We eliminate problem advertisers as soon as we receive customer complaints. Those who appear issue after issue can generally be relied upon to be performing at an acceptable level of customer service.

I just started to collect baseball cards. I want to know how to get good rookie cards such as George Brett, Rod Carew, Steve Carlton, Robin Yount and Don Mattingly. Are starter sets or beginner's packs good for rookie cards?

No. All the cards you'll find in starter sets from dealers, or blister packs at the local toy store, are going to be commons.

I am starting a 1977 Topps set. I don't have much experience collecting older cards and I don't know which ones to get first. Should I get some commons right away or should I go after the stars? How do I collect these cards the cheapest way possible and still get highly-graded specimens?

In building a set — especially an older set — it is always best to buy the most expensive cards first. The superstars and hot rookies are always going to be the cards that go up in price most quickly. By buying the high-value cards first, you will be the one benefiting from any price rise. Also, in the event you give up on your set, you will have high-demand cards that are easier to sell or trade than stacks of commons.

Once you've bought some of the big bucks items, try to acquire a large quantity of the commons. Some of the advertisers in magazines, and occasionally dealers at shows, will offer lots of 100 or more different commons from an older set at an attractive price. It's wise to shop around for a seller who offers the condition you are seeking.

I've seen some dealer advertisements requesting "want lists." There is discussion among my friends as to what should be included in a want list. Can you settle it?

The more the better. When sending a want list to a dealer, the easier you can make it for him to respond, the better your results will be. List the year, issuer, card number and player name of the cards you want. It's also important to indicate the lowest (or highest) grade you will accept. To avoid wasting everybody's time, it's smart to list the price you'll pay. Including a self-addressed stamped envelope will also help your response rate.

How can I tell if a dealer tampers with a wax pack?

You can't tell just by looking at the pack. We once opened a 1975 Topps wax pack that was so badly miswrapped you could see the back of the bottom cards — and still found a Robin Yount rookie inside. Even a tightly-wrapped pack may have been opened and resealed. The only way to tell if a dealer tampers with wax packs is to buy enough of them without getting a major star. But re-

member, you can't expect to find a Don Mattingly rookie in every pack of 1984 cards. With 15 cards in a pack, your chances of getting any particular card in a 660-card set are 1-in-44, or less than one per box.

After buying packs from a shop, I realized they were resealed. What can I do about this, and is it illegal in any way?

Illegal? Not unless they're being offered as "guaranteed unopened." Unethical? Definitely. In most cases, the dealer himself did not open and reseal the wax packs; more often, he unknowingly bought it from someone who did. Either way, we suggest you demand a full refund for the packs from the dealer. If you don't get a refund, never go to his store again. Tell all your friends to do likewise. And then live up to your word.

How do dealers who advertise in your publications acquire the large numbers of single cards they sell? Many will not sell less than 50, 100 or even 500 of a single card. Do factories sell these cards to dealers in bulk?

Yes, but the legitimate card companies make the buyer buy all cards, not just the hot stars and rookies. Dealers who offer mega-card lots may have bought a large number of cases and sorted the cards into singles, or may have purchased the cards they wanted from a wholesaler who has done the sorting.

I have seen ads that are selling "secrets" of how to find the star cards in wax, cello and rack packs. Are these for real?

Yes, they are for real. Baseball cards are packaged in a definite pattern — the cards follow a particular order. The pattern is not 100-percent ironclad, but it's pretty darn close. Usually, wax, cello and rack packs have their own unique pattern.

When I'm at a show, am I allowed to take cards out of their holders to look at them?

With the dealer's permission, you are. We suggest when buying cards that you take them out of whatever kind of holder they're in so you can closely examine them. Sheets and plastic holders can disguise a crease or other imperfection that can only be seen upon closer scrutiny. Some dealers will not let customers take the cards out themselves, but are more than happy to do it for you. Always — this is important — look at the card before you buy it.

How should a price guide be used when buying and selling baseball cards?

Price guides are just what they imply — they are guides, not the end-all to end-alls when it comes to values for cards. Price guides report what individual cards or sets are selling for across the nation at the time the price guide was compiled. The prices are gathered from card shows, auctions and from individual dealers.

But prices vary from region to region. For example, a Don Mattingly card may bring more than "guide price" in New York where Mattingly is popular, whereas in Oakland, Mattingly may sell for well under "guide price."

Card prices on both coasts are generally higher than prices in the Midwest and South. While these factors can account for some discrepancies between actual card values and price guide values, price guides do offer a good ballpark figure for the value of cards.

How can I tell if an autograph or uniform is authentic?

Being able to authenticate these types of items is impossible for most hobbyists. Becoming an expert in autographs or uniforms is an education that takes years and years of handling these items on a daily basis. Fortunately, there are dealers in the hobby who are experts and stand behind the authenticity of their merchandise 100 percent. Also, *Sports Collectors Digest, Card News* and *Baseball Cards* writer Dave Miedema often covers the uniform and autograph hobbies in his columns.

What is especially important when buying these items is to do business with a dealer who is someone highly respected in the field. Talk to other collectors who specialize in uniforms and autographs to find out who to buy from.

Is haggling with a dealer acceptable?

Tactful hagging is quite acceptable. As long as you don't make the dealer a ridiculous offer, there's nothing wrong with trying to get as good of a deal as possible. Remember that a dealer will be more receptive to your offer if you are a good customer or are buying a significant amount of cards.

My father tells me in order to organize a card show at our church I must have a tax number or something to show my profits. Is this true? If so, how do I go about doing this?

The specifics of the taxing and licensing procedure vary from state to state and from city to city. Contact your city attorney and state division of revenue to determine what may be necessary.

Buying, Selling & Trading Cards

I am thinking about becoming a card dealer. Could you give me some tips on how to break into the business?

We suggest you contact the various card companies and request dealer information. The addresses of the major card manufacturers are listed in the "General Information" section in this book. Beyond that, the best advice we can give you is to talk with someone who is already in the business — someone who can give you the nitty-gritty details.

I am thinking about starting my own card shop. Where can I get a dealer's license? What will it cost?

There is no such thing as a hobby dealer's license. You'll have to check your state and local laws concerning business licenses for your locale.

In Canada, cards are difficult to find, so once or twice a year we go to the States to catch up on what we've missed. When we return through customs, sometimes we are charged duty and sometimes we aren't. What's the case?

Enforcement of — and for that matter, knowledge of — custom duty regulation, on both sides of the border, borders on capricious. A Canadian dealer, who regularly does shows in the U.S., tells us that he usually has to pay duty only on unopened Topps cards — because they contain bubble gum and are considered food. Another says he regularly tells the customs people that his whole carload of cards is worth only a couple of hundred dollars and thus pays minimal duty.

We don't have a definitive answer; it looks like whether you pay duty will depend on the particular officer you encounter at the border.

I have been collecting cards in Canada and find it difficult to get certain sets and nearly impossible to buy 10- to 100-card lots of certain players or team sets. I see many ads in magazines, but few have any information about Canadian order, so I'm afraid to order. Writing to each and every advertiser before I order to ask his procedure doesn't work because many times the dealer will be sold out or a rookie will have caught fire and the price will change. What should I do?

Most of the advertisers in the magazines listed in this book are large-scale or full-time dealers who welcome orders from Canada. As a general rule, unless an ad states otherwise, feel free to order with confidence from them.

It will be necessary to obtain a money order at your local bank, denominated in American dollars. You might also check at your post office to see if the postage and insurance fees will be significantly different from those the dealer quoted, and include any difference. If you make it easy for the U.S. dealer to accept your order, most will welcome your business.

HANK Aaron
AUKEE BRAVES OUTFIELD

Errors
&
Variations

Chapter Seven

Variations

Some of the most frequently-asked questions we receive concern errors on baseball cards, with the errors usually occurring on card backs in the statistics or personal data areas. Such errors add nothing to the value of a card. The only time an error is likely to increase a card's value is if the manufacturer corrects the error in a later printing, thus creating two distinct "variations."

If enough people believe the variations are a desirable part of that issue, their value might increase. Whether the error version or corrected version will have the greater value usually depends on the relative scarcity of each card. The more common version will almost always be worth less. So quite often the error can be worth less than the corrected version.

Is there a book that lists all the variations on baseball cards?

Sports Collectors Digest columnist and baseball card error/variation expert Dick Gilkeson has published The Baseball Card Variation Book, Vol. II which is as close to a definitive checklist of baseball card variations that exists. The book sells for $13.95, and can be ordered by writing The Midpointe, 16448 N.W. McNamee Road, Portland, Ore. 97231.

When pricing a set with error cards, how do I estimate the value of the set? Also, how are sets valued in your price guide books and magazines? Do they include the error cards? Corrected versions? Both versions?

Our price guide books and magazines list set prices by using the least expensive variation which may exist in a particular set. Unless the seller states otherwise, always assume when you are buying a set that you will get the least expensive variation of any card. To figure the value of a set that contains the expensive variations, or both variations, add the appropriate single card values to the set price.

Some hobbyists collect sets with all variations. Once complete, these sets are called "master sets." With some sets having more than 30 variations, assembling master sets can be quite challenging.

I bought a Starting Lineup statue of Eric Davis. It has the Eric Davis card, back and cap, but instead of saying "Cincinnati 34" across the chest, it says "Minnesota 34." Is it rare? Have any others turned up?

Somebody at Kenner evidently forgot to switch the chest painting machine from Kirby Puckett to Eric Davis. We haven't heard of any others, so it is undoubtedly rare. That doesn't mean, however, that it has a great deal of value. It takes demand plus scarcity to create value.

I know there are two 1962 Topps #139 Hal Reniff cards. Will you explain the difference between the two?

The scarcer variety pictures Reniff in a hand-above-head pitching pose, while the other photo is a head shot. Another major variation from the 1962 Topps set is Bob Buhl (#458) and Willie Tasby (#462), whose cards come with cap logos (common) or without cap logos (scarcer).

I've been real patient and looked everywhere, so now I'll ask. In the 1991 Bowman, card #246 is Ken Griffey Jr. So why is Ken Griffey Sr. also #246? Was this error corrected?

It is not likely that the numbering was corrected, because of the relatively small press run, but we can't confirm that. The elder Griffey was supposed to be card #255. Unless a Griffey Sr. card #255 was issued, this error will not influence the card's value.

166

*In the 1991 Classic set I found a "Future Aces" card of the young A's pitchers. In the May 1991 issue of **Baseball Cards** magazine you pictured a card that had the title "Four Aces," while ads in the magazine say "Future Aces." How many variations exist?*

Only the "Future Aces" version was issued. The "Four Aces" picture was a preproduction sample provided by Classic.

In the 1969 Topps cards there are many cards listed in the price guides as if there were two different cards, such as 500A Mantle, 500B Mantle (white). The whites are more expensive. Can you explain this to me?

There are 23 cards between #440-511 in the 1969 Topps set on which the player's or players' last name is printed in yellow (common) or white (scarce) letters. All the other cards that have players' last names in white in the 1969 sets come only in white, so they have no premium value.

There are also similar variations in the 1958 Topps set. A total of 33 cards between #2-108 can be found with either yellow or white team or name lettering, with the yellow being the scarcer of the two.

I bought a 1969 Topps white-letter Mickey Mantle variation card. The back of the card is different from all the other 1969 Topps cards I have; there is no copyright line, "T.G.C Printed in U.S.A." Is the Mantle white-letter the only one white-letter variation like this?

It appears to be. None of the several Mantle white-letter cards we've observed has the copyright line, while all the other white-letter variations have it.

What can you tell me about the 1972 Topps green-letter variations?

A handful of the Cubs cards from that year (#18, #29, #45 and #117) can be found with either yellow (common) or green (scarcer) shadows under the letters C and S of the Cubs at the top of the card. The Sports Collectors Digest Baseball Card Price Guide cites a value of $3.50 for the green letters, and 25-50 cents for the yellow letters

I have two different 1973 Topps cards of Twins manager Frank Quilici. On one of the cards, there are trees in the photos behind the portraits of coaches Vern Morgan and Bob Rodgers. On the other card, that area is blank. Is this the only manager's card with this difference?

No. There are similar variations for cards #12 (Padres), #81 (Cubs), #116 (Yankees), #131 (Red Sox), #136 (Orioles), #179 (A's), #237 (Braves), #252 (Giants), #257 (Mets), #486 (Phillies) and #517 (Pirates). The version with the orange background behind the coaches' heads is the more common. There is a small premium on the scarcer variety.

I have a Bump Wills 1979 Topps card in a Texas Rangers uniform but the card says Blue Jays. Is this an error?

Yes. The Wills card from the 1979 Topps set is one of the more well-known errors in recent years. The card that denotes Wills is with the Blue Jays — the error version — is valued at $3 in Near Mint condition; the corrected version, denoting him with the Rangers, is valued at $3.50.

How come Fleer's 1981 Amos Otis card (#483) has "Series Starter" on it instead of his position?

That's one of many variation cards in the 1981 Fleer set. Card #483 features Otis in a batting pose with the "Series Starter" line instead of his position. Card #32 can be found with the identical photo, but his position is listed as "Outfield." There is also a card #32 that has a portrait photo. None of these cards are worth more than 70 cents.

I have a 1981 Fleer Graig Nettles (#87) that has his name on the back as "Craig." Was this ever corrected?

Yes. The "Craig" version, the scarcer of the two, is valued at $12. The "Graig" card is priced at 30 cents.

What does "small hand on back" and "no hand" mean when referring to some cards in the 1981 Fleer set?

On some cards, there is a stray bit of black ink that looks a lot like the outline of a person's hand with the middle finger raised. On the cards of Davey Lopes, Bill Bonham, Ron Cey and Gary Matthews, the finger/hand appears in the lower right corner of some card backs; it's on the white ball on front of the Rick Dempsey and Britt Burns cards. The "hand" versions sell for around $1 each.

I have heard rumors about the 1991 Upper Deck card #246, Frank Thomas, being an error card. His facial expression and right hand look like he is mad at someone and shooting him the bird. If this is an error, could you tell me if it would be worth more than the regular card value and if Upper Deck corrected it?

For what it's worth, we don't think Thomas is flipping off, but even if he were, it would not affect the value of the card unless a new card were issued with a different picture — and that's not going to happen.

While going through my 1982 Topps cards, I noticed a lot of them do not carry players' autographs, just like the George Foster All-Star cards. In the same set, I also have two All-Star cards that carry neither the player's printed name at the bottom of the card or the autograph. Do you have any information on these?

First, none of the All-Star cards in the 1982 Topps are supposed to have autographs. Some Foster cards come that way by mistake, although the corrected version (no autograph) is scarcer and more valuable.

Each of the All-Star cards should have the name printed in black on the bottom; however, a printing press malfunction caused many sheets of the 1982 Topps to be printed without any black ink. It's not very noticeable on the photos, because of the red, blue and yellow inks there, but the missing autograph is the

clue. We've seen some pretty fancy prices for these blackless variations, but we've seen no great evidence of demand by collectors for them.

Then there's the Pascual Perez card from that set, which has the black autograph, but not the black position (pitcher) on the front. The Perez card (#383) is valued at $30.

In price guides, I've seen the 1982 Fleer card #438 listed as All Hrabosky, 5'1", at $20, and the Al Hrabosky, 5'1", at $1.25. My card has his name spelled "Al" and his height at "5' 10". Please set me straight on this card.

Your card is the third printing, corrected version. It is priced as a common.

Why is the 1982 Fleer set worth only $70 when card #576 is worth $175?

The error version of that card, which shows John Littlefield, is not included in the set price. The photo of the error version of the card is from a reversed negative. It shows Littlefield, a right-handed pitcher, throwing left-handed. It's one of the scarcest and most valuable recent variations.

Was the 1982 Fleer card of Lee Smith (#603) corrected with the Cubs logo flipped on the back of the card?

Yes, the logo error was corrected. The error card is the scarcer of the variations.

I discovered a variation in my 1984 send-in glossy cards. About half were printed on white stock and the other half on brown stock. I discovered the same thing on my 1984 Topps All-Star glossies included in the 1985 rack packs. It seems early in the year they were printed on the brown stock and then later switched to the white stock.

Also, on the 1985 rack pack wrappers, I noticed a difference with the change in stocks. The early wrappers with the brown-stock cards said "1984 All-Star Game Commemorative Cards." The later white-stock cards did not have the year printed on them. Another difference on the wrapper was the copyright on the brown-stock cards is 1985 while the wrapper for the white-stock cards is 1986. Do you know which cards and wrappers are least plentiful?

Interesting observations. While we have no way of knowing which color of cardboard or which wrapper is the scarcer, if either, our guess would be that since the rack packs are produced after the wax packs and vending boxes, those wrappers with the 1985 date might be less common. Whether collectors would pay anything extra for these variations in the printing stock is another story.

My 1985 Fleer jersey stickers include two types for the Boston Red Sox. One variety has the city listed, the other says only Red Sox. Is either scarcer than the other?

Probably, but because of lack of collector interest, we'll never know. There are quite a number of variations in the recent Fleer sticker inserts.

I have two 1986 ProCards Tidewater Tides sets that have different logos. One has the Tidewater logo on the front, the other has a Mets logo with two sprouts of water in the foreground. What's the reason for this?

Those aren't two sprouts of water — they're palm trees. That Mets logo is from the Columbia Mets, New York's Double A Southern League affiliate. About half the Tidewater Tides ProCards produced in 1986 have the Columbia logos. The error set is worth $2-$3 more than the corrected set.

Ken Dayley's 1991 Donruss card has a picture of him in a Cardinals uniform, but the team logo on the front is Blue Jays. In the same set, there is a Blue Jay pictured on Bud Black's card, with a Giants logo on the front. Also in the set, the cards of Danny Jackson and Mike Boddicker do not have team logos on the front. Are these error cards?

No. Donruss apparently felt the patches on the uniforms being held by Boddicker and Jackson were adequate substitutes for logos. The Black and Dayley cards were issued too early for Donruss to get photos of the pitchers with their new teams.

In 1986, the Leukemia Society of America offered an autographed Gary Carter baseball card for a $10 donation. The card is a 1986 Topps All-Star card (#708)

171

with a difference. It has a non-glossy front, but instead of using a grey cardboard for the back, it has white stock like the Tiffany glossy series. The New York Mets newspaper says Topps specially printed only 6,000 of these for the charity. Would this card be considered a true variation?

Yes, but since it has received little publicity, there has been no great demand for it.

I own a 1986 Donruss card #567 of Joel Youngblood that lists his position as pitcher. I know he's not a pitcher. Was this error ever corrected?

Yes, it was. The scarcer variety lists Youngblood's position as infield on the card front.

The front of David Palmer's 1986 Donruss card (#254) lists him as a second baseman, but he is a pitcher. Was this corrected? Is it valuable?

The Palmer error, found in 1986 Donruss wax packs, was corrected in the subsequent printing of factory-collated sets sold through hobby dealers. Because there are fewer corrected versions, it is more valuable ($1) than the error card (six cents).

I have two 1987 Sportflics Steve Garvey cards (#40). One has a copyright date line of 1986 in the lower right corner. The other has no copyright. Is this a variation?

Yes, but since few people (if any) collect Sportflics' many copyright variations, it hasn't yet added any value to the card.

Could you explain the variations on Cory Synder's 1987 Sportflics card (#24)?

There are three versions of the card. The first has a Pat Tabler photo on the card back (Tabler facing front) with a ¼-swing depicted on the card front; the second has Tabler on the back (facing front) with a ½-swing on the front; the third, the correct card, has the Snyder photo on the back (facing to the side). The cards with Tabler backs are valued at $2 each, while the card with Snyder is priced at $1.

While looking at my 1987 Topps set, I noticed the Dwight Gooden and Don Mattingly All-Star cards, Lance Parrish (#791), George Bell (#681) and Luis Aquino (#301), are without the trademark logo on the card fronts. Were these cards ever corrected?

Only the Urbano Lugo (#92), Dwight Gooden All-Star (#603) and Don Mattingly All-Star (#606) cards without trademarks were corrected. Other variations from the 1987 Topps issue are: #344 Joe Niekro with the copyright line either inside or outside the yellow printing on the back; and #671 Roy Soff with or without the "D" before the copyright line.

I have five 1990 Donruss All-Star cards — Ryne Sandberg, Mark McGwire, Wade Boggs, Ozzie Smith and Benito Santiago. On the backs it says "Recent Major League Performance" instead of "All-Star Game Performance." Why aren't they listed as errors?

Our price guide doesn't list "errors;" it lists cards with premium value. Most collectors are not willing to pay a premium for these cards, although they are scarcer than their corrected versions.

I have a 1990 Bo Jackson All-Star card. It has no "TM" on the American League symbol on the bottom right. Why isn't it listed in your price guide?

Because nobody will pay a premium price for the card. The only error and variation cards we list are those with a premium value.

One of my Mike Scioscia 1991 Donruss All-Star cards (#436) has a yellow star, the other has a white star. Is this an error or variation, and will it have any extra value?

It's a legitimate variation, but since few collectors get excited about minor variations on current cards, it's unlikely to attain much premium value.

I purchased some 1987 Donruss Opening Day team sets of the Pittsburgh Pirates. I have two different Barry Bonds cards. One shows him in the normal white jersey, the other shows him in a black batting practice jersey. Could you tell me why?

You have one of the most valuable variations in many years. The "Bonds" card in the black jersey is actually Johnny Ray; the white jersey card is Bonds. The black-jersey card is listed at $125 in Mint condition.

I have a factory sealed 1987 Donruss Opening Day set. How do I tell if I have the set with the Barry Bonds error on it?

The only way to find out is to open the set.

In my collection, I found a 1988 Topps Ed Correa card (#227) without the row of white baseballs on the back by his name. Is this an error?

It appears to be a legitimate printing variation. The same variation has been noted on several other 1988 Topps cards.

Checklist 397-528 in my 1988 Topps set lists card #455 as Steve Carlton. I don't remember seeing a Carlton card. My card #455 is Shawn Hillegas. What's going on?

Topps originally planned to include Carlton in its 1988 set, but since it appeared he might retire, the company replaced him with Hillegas before production began. However, it neglected to correct the checklist until later in the press run. There are now two checklist cards — one listing card #455 as Carlton and another as Hillegas.

I have two different 1988 Topps special offer insert cards that are found in wax packs. One has a black arrow located in the lower right corner and the other has no arrow. Is one more valuable than the other?

Actually, the insert card can be found in three varieties: 1) black arrow in corner; 2) words "Cards Not Included" in corner; and 3) no words or arrow in corner. Variety #2 seems to be the least abundant. Lack of collector interest in current insert cards will prevent any of them from having substantial value.

The 1988 Topps set I have has an Eddie Murray Record Breaker card (#4) with three lines of boxed type on the front. I know some Murray cards do not contain the box. Which is the scarcer version?

The Murray card with the boxed type on the front is the scarcer version. Its value is $1.25 in Mint condition.

There are two variations of Mark McGwire's 1988 Topps Record Breaker card (#3). One has a white triangle behind his left foot, the other doesn't. Which is rarer?

The cards were produced in about equal proportion; the triangle card may be found slightly less often.

I have seen the 1988 Topps Keith Comstock error card (white team name) #778 at $4, while his regular card (blue team name) is only worth 25 cents. The only difference in the cards is the color of the team name. Why does this error make the card so valuable?

The error doesn't make the card valuable; the fact that a corrected version was issued does. The correction created two distinct variations of the card. Many collectors feel they need both versions to have a complete 1988 Topps set. Since the white-letter card is much scarcer than the blue-letter card, it sells for more.

175

I have noticed in the 1989 Fleer set the backs of the Tom Brookens and Mike Heath cards are transposed. Were these cards corrected?

Yes. Fleer did correct the flip-flopped backs on these cards. Minor errors are not usually corrected, but Fleer deemed these mistakes significant enough to rectify. It should be pointed out that the back of the error cards are not completely wrong. The card numbers are correct, but the player name and all additional information are not.

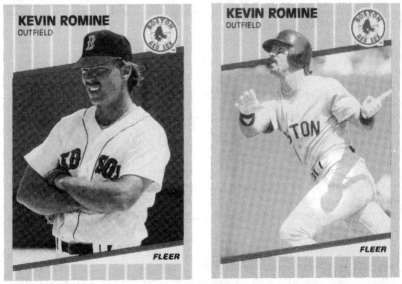

I have found two versions of the 1989 Fleer Kevin Romine card (#98). One

shows a player swinging a bat, the other shows him standing with his arms folded. What do you know about this?

The version showing the player swinging the bat is not Romine; it's Randy Kutcher. The corrected version shows Romine.

I have a 1990 Donruss MVP card of John Smoltz, but the photo is Tom Glavine. Is it worth much?

The Glavine photo error is listed at $2 in the sixth annual price guide, but you should be able to buy it much cheaper from a seller who isn't familiar with the Braves pitchers.

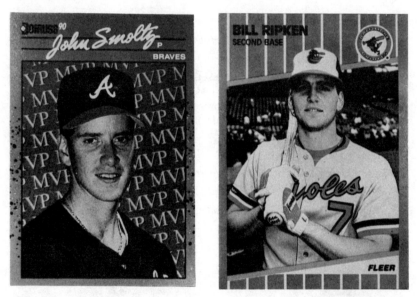

How many different variations were created for the 1989 Fleer Billy Ripken card?

We recognize six variations of the infamous Ripken card: 1) obscenity; 2) obscenity blocked out with rectangular box; 3) obscenity scratched out; 4) obscenity scratched out, with a loop in the scratch-out; 5) obscenity airbrushed out; 6) obscenity with slit (the slit can be easily faked).

The 1989 Donruss checklist card #600 has two versions — one spells Curt Schilling's name correctly, the other misspells his name as Kurt. Would this error be more valuable because it was corrected?

It may be someday, but historically, variations on checklist cards generate little demand from collectors.

Errors & Variations

While looking at the 1989 Topps "Future Stars" cards, I noticed that the borders around the players' photos are two different sizes. Could you comment on these variations?

The 1989 "Future Star" cards are found with two different croppings (the way the photos were sized for the cards). However, there seems to be little collector interest. We don't feel the variations will catch on to the point that either will ever be worth much more than the other.

I have numerous 1989 Topps rack packs with Gregg Jefferies and Gary Sheffield on the backs. Is there any way I can tell which version of these Future Star cards I have without opening them?

Nope.

My 1989 Topps Gary Sheffield card has what looks like the number "43" in the lower-left corner. What is this?

Since Sheffield's card is #343 in the set, we think the dot-matrix number in the corner is some sort of production code overprinted on the original photo prior to the beginning of the printing process. Later printings of the card show that Topps re-bordered the photo to hide the number, creating the variation you mentioned.

What's all this talk about the 1989 Upper Deck Ken Griffey Jr., error? Does it have something to do with the border?

Yes. The so-called "error" card is ⅟₁₆" taller than the other cards.

Ken Griffey Jr.

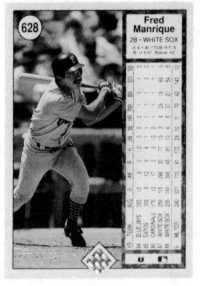

178

Which of the 1989 Upper Deck Fred Manrique cards (#628) is correct and which is the error? The photo on the back of one card has him throwing a ball and the other version shows him hitting.

The error card is one showing the player throwing — that is shortstop Ozzie Guillen, not Manrique.

Reversed or "Flopped" Negatives

Hank Aaron's 1957 Topps card shows him batting lefty. Wasn't Aaron a right-handed batter?

Yes. Topps reversed the negative when it printed Aaron's 1957 card (#20). The card was not corrected, so there's no additional premium on an already expensive ($225) card.

I have a 1969 Topps card of Seattle Pilots catcher Larry Haney (#209). He is pictured as a left-handed catcher. Is this card of any value?

The 1969 Haney error card is of no value higher than common card price. The negatives used for the photo were unintentionally reversed for the 1969 card. Interestingly, the very same photo appears on Haney's 1968 Topps card, when he was with the Orioles, but it is printed correctly.

ELSTON HOWARD
CATCHER

DON LARSON
PITCHER

After sorting some wax packs of "Baseball Legends" cards, I noticed I had two Elston Howard cards. On one, he is facing left, and on the other, he is facing right. Which is correct? Is it considered a major error of any value?

The card which shows Howard with the catcher's mitt on his left hand is correct; the other is a reversed negative. There were a number of misspelled names and other errors in this collectors issue which were corrected. There is currently little or no premium on any of the cards in this set — error or corrected.

On Jim Gantner's 1987 Topps card (#108), the Brewers logo on his cap is backwards. How come? Was it corrected?

The Gantner photo is the result of flopped negatives in the preprinting production process, resulting in a mirror image. It was not corrected.

I found an error in the 1989 Fleer "Baseball Superstars" set. Kal Daniels' card shows him batting right-handed. Also, the "C" on his helmet is backwards. Was this error corrected?

No, so it adds no value to the card. The Fleer boxed sets are generally produced in such limited quantities that there is no chance to correct any errors that may be discovered.

The 1989 Score card of Ray Knight (#135) says he throws right, but on the front of the card, he has a glove on his right hand. Is this new to anyone?

It was to Score. The Knight card was originally issued with a flopped photo that made the third baseman appear to be left-handed. That was corrected and the photo was changed to show him as a righty. The lefty card is scarcer.

How can you tell the error 1989 Upper Deck Dale Murphy card?

181

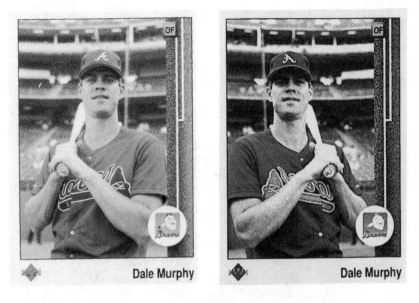

The error is a reversed photo. The easiest way to remember is that the error card shows Murphy with the bat over his left shoulder. The bat is over his right shoulder on the corrected card. The error card carries a value of $60.

Blank Backs/Wrong Backs & Other Printing Errors

Another frequently-asked question deals with current or recent (1980s) cards which have wrong backs (player on the front doesn't match the biography/statistics on the back), or blank backs (no printing on back). Such cards result from the printing process and aren't very popular with collectors, so they have little, if any, premium value. Most collectors view these types of cards to be damaged, and value them lower than correctly-printed specimens. The only exception seems to be currently hot superstar or rookie cards, for which a few collectors are willing to pay premiums, sometimes as high as $10.

I have a 1941 Play Ball with a Bill Dickey front and Dolph Camilli back. Are wrong backs from this era scarce and do they have any value?

Wrongbacks from the 1939-1941 Play Ball set are found on occasion. Many collectors would consider wrong backs from those sets unique items. A Dickey card in Excellent condition sells for $325. We'd guess a Dickey wrong back would at least bring that much and perhaps a bit more.

I have some 1982 Topps and Fleer cards that have well-centered fronts, but the backs have halves of two different cards. Do these have any premium value?

Most collectors consider these cards to be miscuts, and worth less than correctly cut cards.

I have a 1982 Topps Traded card (#103) of Steve Sax with a double signature on it. I would like to know if this is an error, and if it is, was it corrected?

We've never heard of the double signature on this card. If you mean there are two complete signatures on the card, look closely and you'll find that one of them is the work of somebody practicing their forgery. If you mean there is a double printing in the area of the signature, it probably indicates a printing mistake. In the first case, the card is totally ruined; in the second instance, it is almost totally ruined.

I found a 1985 Fleer Don Sutton card with Tom Tellman's stats printed over Sutton's stats. Would this effect the value of the card?

Yes, it lowers it. Nobody collects this type of printing mistake. Or if they do collect them, they don't pay a premium for them.

I have noticed something strange on the back of one of my 1985 Topps #1 Draft Pick cards, #280 Shawon Dunston. It does not have the green ink that makes up the border on the back and frames the #1. Does this make the card more valuable?

The card's value isn't enhanced.

I saw a 1986 Donruss Highlights Darryl Strawberry card that had the "Highlight" logo on the card front in white instead the yellow. The dealer said it was "very rare." Do you know how many of these errors have been noticed and if they have any value?

While this is a legitimate — and rare — variation, almost no one collects Donruss Highlights sets, so the card currently has no great value.

I opened a 1986 Fleer wax box and found a dozen or so cards without the yellow ink on the back. Since this isn't a blank back or wrong back, would it be considered a variation?

Errors & Variations

No. It falls under the heading of a printing error. Color changes which are the result of deliberate design changes, such as the 1958 yellow letter, 1969 white letter, and 1972 green letter variations are another matter, creating collectible variations which carry a premium value.

In my 1986 Sportflics set, about 20 have parts of all three photos which remain present no matter how the card is tilted. Are these cards valuable or worthless?

Due to a printing flaw, the triple-action process on your card cannot be completed. We consider the cards to be worthless.

I got 1986 Topps Dwight Gooden card (#250) that had the Mets name at the top and the position circle at the bottom in red, instead of the usual orange. I went to a show and showed this card to various dealers who said there is no value to it, though none of them could tell me why. The 1982 Topps error card of Pascual Perez is worth $35, and this Gooden card has the same kind of error. Could it be that this card was being presented from the wrong side of the table? Or is it really of no value?

While your Gooden card may have some curiosity value, it really does not have any premium value. The difference between it and the no-position Perez is that the Perez card "error" was apparently the fault of omission in the preparation of the card for printing while your Gooden "error" was caused by a printing press goof.

You might say it is a case of design "error" — the omission of the word "Pitcher" from the card design of Perez — versus a mechanical error — the failure of the printing press to put the yellow ink into the area described. These are fine lines of distinction, but they seem to be the ones collectors use when determining whether an "error" card carries any extra value. Generally, the rule of thumb is this: If the variation is caused by anything up to the stage of the actual printing, it will have significantly more premium than a version which is the result of a printing mistake.

I have a 1986 Topps wax pack card panel with Reggie Jackson, Don Mattingly, Oddibe McDowell and Willie McGee, but the backs have Jorge Bell, Wade Boggs, George Brett and Vince Coleman. Have you had any reports of boxes like this? Do you think this box is worth a nice amount?

Frankly, we don't think it's worth a really big premium, although perhaps a buyer could be found at three to five times the value of a normal bottom panel. Considering the relatively low number of box bottoms in circulation, we have had quite a few reports of wrong-back errors, so we wonder just how rare they really are. In short, it's a nice item, but with more curiosity value than collector appeal.

I purchased two 1987 Columbus Clippers TCMA sets. In one set, I found the Orestes Destrade card (#13) missing his name and position. Has anyone else found similar variations in the set?

Not to our knowledge. It sounds as though the black ink was left off the card in the printing process.

I have a 1987 Donruss Mike Greenwell card (#585) with a small red stripe on his right sleeve. Since I have seen no others like this, I must ask if it is an error card.

No, it's a printing flaw. A significant percentage of the 1987 Donruss Greenwells evidence this flaw, but that does not make it a true variation. Most collectors would value it lower than a perfectly-printed card.

I bought the 1987 Donruss baseball card set for my collection. When I was going through them, picking out the few cards I already had, I found I had one card of Bill Madlock (#155) with the regular brown stripe behind his name, and one with a red stripe. What can you tell me about this?

Without having seen the card, we'd guess the red-stripe card was printed without one of the four primary colors. This happens from time to time. Look closely at the other colors on the card with the red stripe. If they don't match up, a color was probably missed. If that's the case, it's an accident in the printing process, and as a result, the card has no additional premium value.

I believe I discovered an error card in the 1987 Topps set. On the back of Andres Thomas' card (#296), there's an editor's note, under the statement on Nolan Ryan's no-hitter, saying "Nolan Ryan's fifth...". That's the correct version. The error version says, "Nolan Ryan's pifth..." Now, since this error was corrected, it has to be worth more, right?

Wrong. Taking a close look at the two photocopies you sent us, the "P" doesn't appear to be a "P" at all — at least is doesn't look like the other Ps on the editor's notes on other cards. It looks like a messed-up "F." Our guess is a piece of stray type wandered onto the card during the printing process. Printing foulups like these are not considered errors, so the card has no additional value.

I noticed on some of the 1987 Topps Royals Leaders cards (#256), there is a squiggly line over the card number. I know this was corrected. Will these cards be worth anything?

We looked at the few duplicate Royals Leaders cards we had and did not discover a squiggly line variation. But we don't doubt what you've told us. In the past, printing flaws of this nature have received little or no publicity — and the flawed cards have developed no additional value.

I have a 1987 Topps Don Mattingly card which has part of another card showing on the front. Is it worth keeping or should we trash it?

If it was anybody but a top star or hot rookie, a card this badly miscut would be worthless. If you tried hard and long enough, you might be able to find a buyer for this aberration.

I have a 1987 Donruss Rated Rookie card of Benito Santiago that is printed upside-down. Would that have any premium value?

All 1987 (and 1988) Donruss cards can be found with this variation. The cards printed for wax packs, etc., have the ball with the card number in the upper right when the card is flipped over. The cards printed for factory sets have the backs upside-down. Some superstar fanatics may feel they have to buy both versions of their favorite player's card.

Also, you might notice the factory set cards are ever-so slightly smaller than the wax pack cards. That's the result of an extra trimming process to make them more uniform. In and of themselves, these differences add no value to single cards, although some people attach a higher value to a complete factory set than to a hand-collated set.

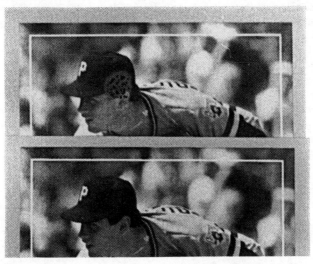

I have a 1988 Score card of Mike Bielecki with a faded spot over his right ear. I

have others without the faded spot. Is this an error?

It's a printing flaw. As such, it detracts, rather than adds to, the value of a card. A similar flaw can be found on some of the 1989 Donruss cards of Eric Hetzel.

I bought a few 1988 Fleer wax packs, and found a Gregg Jefferies and a Mike Greenwell card which were in black-and-white. Plus, the Fleer logo was missing from the lower right-hand corner. Have you seen or heard of these errors?

Your cards sound like printing mistakes. As such, most collectors would place no premium value. However, since the mistakes sound like they give the cards a very dramatic appearance, and since the cards are of currently popular players, you might be able to find a buyer willing to pay more than guide value for them.

I have two different 1988 Topps Ted Higuera cards. One has the team name in red, the other in orange. Is one of my cards a hard-to-find variation?

No. Most differences in shades of a color on modern baseball cards can be traced to the printing operation, rather than design of the card.

I have three boxes of 1988 Topps cards with misprinted wrappers. The large "Topps" at the top of the ball is missing, and "1988" is white instead of blue. Have you heard of any other wax packs like this?

No, but since it is more likely a printing error rather than a design variation, don't look for a significant premium value.

I found variations in all 12 1989 Donruss "Grand Slammer" cards. Each of the cards can be found with five different color bands at top. One dealer tells me these were produced illegally and Donruss is trying to recall all cello packs and cases containing these cards. Is that true?

The "dealer" who told you that doesn't know what he's talking about. The color variations are a result of the way the subset was printed. They will add no value to the card.

I saw some 1989 Upper Deck cards missing the hologram on the back. Are these rare?

No. After the missing hologram cards came on the market, some dealers were asking and getting big prices for them. But the missing hologram can be easily faked.

I have a 1990 Upper Deck Kevin Seitzer card that has two holograms on the back. Neither of the holograms is in the right spot. Will the printing error increase the value of the card?

Maybe some day, but not yet. Most collectors think Upper Deck cards with misplaced holograms are just damaged cards and are unwilling to pay a premium price for them.

I have a 1989 Upper Deck Ellis Burks with no name printed on the front. Could you tell me if there are any more cards like this, and what is the current value?

We can make you all the no-name Upper Deck cards you like. Because of high quality finish on the cardboard stock on which they are printed, the ink on Upper Deck cards can easily be removed with an eraser. Such phony variations are worthless.

Common Errors

	Games	At Bat	Runs	Hits	2b	3b	H.R.	R.B.I.	B.Avg	P.O.	Assists	Errors	F.Avg
Year	124	474	48	121	23	11	5	47	.255	253	18	6	.978
Life	87	148	27	38	5	3	2	12	.257	81	1	1	.988

I noticed that the lifetime stats on the back of Roberto Clemente's 1956 Topps card are lower than those for the previous year. Why is this? Is this an error?

Yes. The line for the previous season's statistics actually reflects Clemente's 1954 performance at Montreal, in the Dodgers' minor league organization. The lifetime stat line is his 1955 rookie year performance in the big leagues.

The back of my 1965 Topps Jim Hunter card has his name spelled "Tim" Hunter. Was this corrected?

No.

I have read about the 1969 Topps card of Aurelio Rodriguez (#653) that actually has a photo of the team batboy. I have searched all over North Carolina trying to find it. Could you give me more information on it and tell me why it is so hard to find? What is it worth?

The card does, in fact, picture Angels batboy Leonard Garcia, who conspired with Rodriguez to trick the photographer. The card, valued at $1.50 in Near Mint, is not rare, but because it is part of the scarcer high-number series of 1969 Topps, can be difficult to locate.

I purchased a 1966 Topps Jim Palmer rookie card. The brief biography on the card back says Palmer is a left-hander. That statement, of course, is wrong. Was this error ever corrected?

189

Errors & Variations

No, it was not corrected. Another error can be found on the card, too. Palmer's lifetime ERA after the 1965 season was 3.72, not 3.82.

On the back of the 1967 Topps Whitey Ford card (#5) it reads 1933 instead of 1953 in his career statistics. Is this a recognized error?

This mistake has been documented in the past. The error was never corrected and the card has no additional value.

On Nolan Ryan's 1981 Donruss card, under the 1979 stats, it says he signed with the Houston "Atros." Was this incorrect spelling ever corrected?

No. Although there were many 1981 Donruss variations created by correcting errors on the backs of cards, the Ryan card was not one of them.

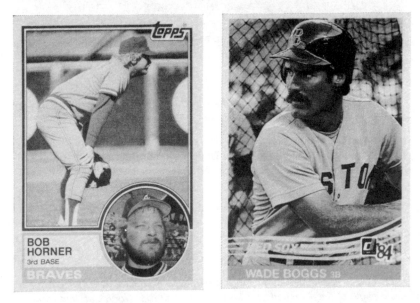

My 1983 Topps Bob Horner card says he had 32 home runs and seven RBI in 1982. Was this error ever corrected by Topps?

It was not corrected. And by the way, Horner had 97 RBI in 1982.

I have a 1984 Donruss #151 Wade Boggs. On the stat side, under the runs column, it says he scored only 10 times in 1983, when actually he scored 100 runs. I'm wondering if this is like this on all of the 1984 Donruss cards, or whether there it is a misprint on only a small number of cards.

All of the cards contain the error, so it adds no value to the card.

My 1990 Upper Deck extended Cecil Fielder card #786 does not have 1989 stats on the back. Is this an error? Has it been corrected? Does it have any value?

The 1990 Upper Deck high-number Cecil Fielder card doesn't have 1989 stats on the back because Fielder spent that season playing pro ball in Japan. It's not an error; it was not corrected and it doesn't add any value to the card.

I have found in the 1990 Upper Deck baseball some cards #101-199 without the copyright printed on them. Would these be something collectors would look for?

Only the most devoted variation collector would be interested. Each of the cards in that number range (they're all printed on one sheet) can be found with and without copyright. The missing copyright currently adds no value to the cards.

The back of Jeff Reardon's 1985 Leaf card says he had only two career losses, but the stats shown add up to 27. Was this error corrected?

No. So there's no premium value.

I recently purchased a 1986 Donruss Vince Coleman card (#181) and noticed his batting average is 2.67. Was this mistake corrected?

No, it was not.

On the 1986 Topps card of Ryne Sandberg, the word "Topps" is missing on the front. Was this ever corrected?

No.

Dale Sveum was on the Topps All-Star Rookie team in 1987, yet none of my 1987 Topps cards have the Topps All-Star Rookie trophy pictured. Is this an error?

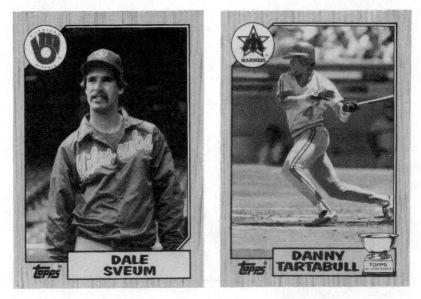

Yes, but since no Sveum cards were issued with the trophy, there is no premium value.

I noticed an error on Glenn Davis' 1987 Topps card (#560). His major league home run total is given as 54, but the yearly figures add up to 53. Was this error ever corrected to change the value of the card?

Your math is better than Topps' math. And no, the error was not corrected.

My 1988 Topps Traded card of Jim Abbott doesn't have the red and blue stripes in the last period of U.S.A. Was this corrected?

No, so it adds no value to the card.

The back of Scott Fletcher's 1988 Score card says he played his first four years with the White Sox, but yet the stats say he was a member of the Cubs. Which was right, and was the mistake corrected?

Fletcher played with the White Sox. The error was not corrected.

The 1989 Fleer checklist shows Houston Astros cards #367 and #368 are Nolan Ryan and Mike Scott, respectively. My Mike Scott card, however, is #367. Is it an error?

Yes, to the extent that Fleer usually numbers its cards alphabetically within a team. The checklist was not corrected.

On the back of Jose Canseco's 1989 Donruss Grand Slammer it says he hit his 1988 World Series grand slam in the second game and was followed by Kirk Gi-

bson's home run in the ninth inning. Both were hit in Game 1. Does the card have a variation?

No.

Oddities, Not Errors

While going through some old cards, I found some 1970 Topps cards with team names in yellow and team names in white. Was this an error?

No. Unlike some years of Topps cards, team names on the 1970 cards are not color consistent. Most can be found in black, white, red and yellow, depending on the background of the card photo.

What is the difference between the Donruss Diamond King puzzle pieces with periods and the ones without periods next to the number?

If you mean the price difference, there is none — they are both worthless.

I have a 1978 Topps Reggie Jackson card. On the back it says, "Reggie's 2-run homer in the 9th inning helped the Yankees beat Bosox 9-14-77." Bosox should be Boston. Does this card have any additional value?

No, because Bosox is a perfectly-acceptable contraction of Boston Red Sox. Just so you know, here are some other acceptable contractions you may run across: Chisox and Pale Hose for White Sox; Redlegs for Reds; Redbirds for Cardinals; M's for Mariners; Phils for Phillies; O's and Birds for Orioles; Bengals for Tigers; Halos for Angels; Jays for Blue Jays; Yanks for Yankees; and Bucs for Pirates.

I have Lou Piniella's 1979 Topps card #648. On the back of the card it has #18. Would this error increase the card's value?

We occasionally receive letters from collectors who are positive they've discovered a variation in a late-1970s Topps set. What those collectors really have are cards from the Burger King sets issued from 1977-1980. The cards were produced by Burger King for Topps and do not contain any type of Burger King identification.

Many of the cards in the Burger King sets are identical to the Topps cards of that year, with only the numbering being different. Eight Burger King sets featuring the Astros, Phillies, Rangers, Tigers and Yankees were issued during the 1977-1980 period. Your Piniella card is a Burger King card. Checklists for the Burger King sets can be found in the sixth edition of the *SCD Baseball Card Price Guide.*

Errors & Variations

The 1985 Donruss card of Danny Jackson does not look like him, and the player is pitching right-handed. Who is the pitcher?

For some time it was thought the pitcher shown was Steve Farr, but a minor league official identified the player as Frank Wills. Incorrect player photos on cards seems to happen at least once a year.

I have a question about George Bell. I have a couple of cards, such as 1985 and 1986 Topps, on which his name is spelled "Jorge." I also have a 1986 Donruss which is spelled "George." Which is right? Is one of them an error?

On his 1982 rookie cards, Topps, Fleer and Donruss all spelled Bell's name as Jorge. He did not appear in any of the 1983 sets, and when he returned in 1984, Fleer and Donruss used his preferred anglicized spelling of George, while Topps clung to the Jorge version until 1987. None of these can be considered errors.

Tony Fernandez's 1987 Topps card says he played 163 games in 1986. How is that possible in a 162-game season? Is this an error?

No error. If a player appears in a game that ends in a rained-out tie, the individual stats count, although the game itself doesn't.

Three of the cards (possibly more) in the 1987 Topps set have an "On This Date" feature on the back that says Mike Paxton, Bill Bonham and Phil Niekro each struck out four batters in an inning. Is this a misprint?

No misprint. It's possible to strike out four (or more) batters in an inning. If the catcher drops a third strike, the batter can still run to first base. The pitcher still gets credit for the strikeout.

194

I have two 1988 Donruss checklist cards (#300). One starts at #240, the other at #248. Are either of these errors?

No. The list starting with #248 is the list found in packs of Donruss cards, the other list was issued with the factory set.

I recently bought the 1988 Score set. I noticed that the card of Tom Hume (#494) lists his team as the Reds, yet Hume is wearing a Phillies uniform. Is this an error?

No, not really. It's not unusual for a card company to picture a player in a uniform of a former team, especially if the player was recently traded. The card companies normally shoot all of their player photos in spring training. They do not run out to shoot a new photo every time a player changes teams during the baseball season and insert it into their regular sets (although traded sets include players with their new teams).

In this instance, Hume was signed by the Reds on Aug. 18, 1987, after being released by the Phillies on Aug. 10. To prepare for its 1988 set, Score evidently took player photos prior to Aug. 10, 1987.

I don't see a trademark by the words "Rated Rookie" on Nelson Liriano's 1988 Donruss card (#32). Is this an error?

No, because the "TM" letters are there. They're hidden in the dark background on this card, and several other 1988 Donruss Rated Rookies.

The 1989 Upper Deck card of Mark Grant shows him on the front as a left-

195

handed pitcher, and on the back as a righty. The back also says he throws right-handed. The photo on the front is not reversed, since the letters on his uniform read correctly. Why would he be pictured as a lefty?

Grant was playing "fool the photographer." Every so often, a player pulls this trick.

I have a 1989 Fleer card of George Brett which says he played for Omaha in 1973. All my other Brett cards say he played for the Royals in 1973. Was this an error?

No. You'll notice he played most of the season with Omaha, then came up to the majors with Kansas City. Most of the other card companies don't include minor league stats.

I just noticed the insert card in 1989 Topps wax packs that offers the glossy send-away cards has "R. Raines" instead of "T. Raines." Will this be corrected?

No, because the 1989 Topps card of Tim Raines has his nickname, "Rock," on front and back.

The back of the 1972 Reggie Jackson "In Action" card has a story about Hank Aaron's 600th home run. Is this a wrong back?

No. Your card carries the correct card number, #436. The backs of the 1972 "In Action" cards had a lot of odd things that didn't pertain to the player pictured on the front.

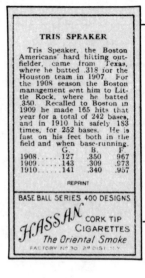

Reprints, Collectors' Issues & Counterfeits

Chapter Eight
Reprints

How can I tell if a card is a reprint?

Usually, a reprinted card will state somewhere on the card that it is a reprint (usually on the card back). Reprint sets aren't meant to fool the buyer into believing he is buying the real McCoy; rather, they are a substitute for cards the collector would normally not be able to afford. Physical differences between reprints and original cards include gloss, thickness of cardboard and size. Some of the major sets that have been reprinted include the 1910 T-206, 1940 Play Ball, 1948 and 1951 Bowman, and the 1952 Topps.

Has anyone ever done a reprint of the N-172 Old Judge cards of the 1880s?

Yes. In the late 1970s, a collector made some photographic reprints of a couple of dozen Old Judge cards. All are from the series which includes a white "O" card number on the front. The reprints are somewhat smaller than the originals, and the photos are not as sharp.

197

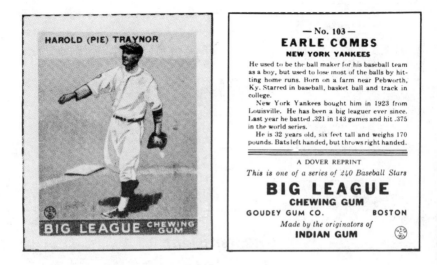

— No. 103 —
EARLE COMBS
NEW YORK YANKEES

He used to be the ball maker for his baseball team as a boy, but used to lose most of the balls by hitting home runs. Born on a farm near Pebworth, Ky. Starred in baseball, basket ball and track in college.

New York Yankees bought him in 1923 from Louisville. He has been a big leaguer ever since. Last year he batted .321 in 143 games and hit .375 in the world series.

He is 32 years old, six feet tall and weighs 170 pounds. Bats left handed, but throws right handed.

A DOVER REPRINT
This is one of a series of 240 Baseball Stars
BIG LEAGUE
CHEWING GUM
GOUDEY GUM CO.   BOSTON
Made by the originators of
INDIAN GUM

I bought a Pie Traynor Gum Co. card at a flea market for 15 cents. Its edges are perforated, but "Copyright 1933" is written on the back, so I'm not sure if it is old or a remake.

It's a modern replica with no collector value. The giveaway is the line at the bottom that says "A DOVER REPRINT." Also, original DeLong cards of 1933 do not have glossy fronts or perforated edges. Your card came from a book of reprints.

What can you tell me about this 1933 Goudey Napoleon (Larry) Lajoie card I bought?

The card you sent, which reads "Napoleon Lajoie Value $7,500 1933 Goudey Gum" on the back, is not a 1933 Goudey Gum Lajoie, and not worth $7,500. It's a modern reprint worth a few cents. The original Lajoie is one of the scarcest cards in the hobby, and is valued at $30,000 in top shape. This card was not really part of the 1933 set, but was added after collectors complained card #106 was missing. Collectors had to write in to get the card, but since the company never advertised that fact, very few people actually wrote in.

How can I tell the difference between the original 1952 Topps and the reprint set?

The most obvious is the difference in size. The original cards measured 2⅝" by 3¾", and the reprints are 2½ by 3½". Also, "Topps 1952 Reprint Series" is stated on the card backs of the reprints.

I heard that the company that printed the 1981 Nashville Sounds-Arby's set with Don Mattingly printed extra sets after the price went up. Is that true?

Yes. The team ordered the set reprinted when it hit the $100 value. It was selling the reprint to collectors for $50. There is no way to tell the reprint from the original, so the whole project had the effect of lowering the value of all sets.

Collectors' Issues

What is a collectors' issue?

It is a card made to be sold directly to collectors rather than issued as a premium for another product. Collectors' issues are not usually legitimate issues. Very often these cards show nothing but the player's photo and his name on the front, and his name and perhaps a line or two of statistics on the back. The sets have names such as "Action All-Stars" or "Big League All-Stars," but usually lack a manufacturer's name. They are sold at shops and shows and carry high price tags.

These cards can be printed and reprinted at will, so they lack any scarcity value. They are not licensed by Major League Baseball or the players' association. All Krause Publications magazines and books refuse to carry advertising for these cards, and do not mention them in stories.

I have 16 stickers of big name stars of the 1960s. I would like some information concerning their background.

You have a recent unauthorized, miniaturized sticker version of the star players from the 1966 Coca-Cola postcard issue. While the original postcards are scarce and collectible, your stickers have no collector value.

I have a black-and-white Don Mattingly card that pictures him with the Columbus Clippers in an old-time uniform. It has his 1982 and 1983 stats on the back, but does not give a company name. Can you tell me more about it?

This is an unauthorized collectors' issue printed in 1986. As such, it has no premium value since the dealer who printed them is free to reprint them anytime demand increases.

I recently bought a black-and-white Don Mattingly card that lists his team as Reitz Memorial Tigers. The dealer said it was Don's high school card. What can you tell me about the card?

We can tell you the card is an unauthorized collectors' issue designed to line the pockets of the person who ripped-off the picture from the July, 16, 1979,

REITZ MEMORIAL TIGERS

DON MATTINGLY   OF - P

REITZ MEMORIAL TIGERS
DON MATTINGLY

Home: Evansville, Ind.

Born: 4-20-61

Bats: Left   Throws: Left

Weight: 180

Height: 5'11"

In his past two seasons, Don batted .500 and .552.

Don belted 140 RBIs in four years for the Tigers, tying the record in scholastic baseball.

DON MATTINGLY
EVANSVILLE, IND.

Mattingly, 18, an outfielder-pitcher, batted .500 and .552 over the past two seasons to lead Reitz Memorial High to a 59–1 record. He had 140 RBIs in four years for the Tigers, equaling the highest total ever in scholastic baseball.

issue of *Sports Illustrated.* It was distributed through the network of people who handle such junk cards. It has no collector value and never will.

I bought a black-and-white Mark McGwire card. The dealer said it was his college card. It has "Glacier Pilots, Anchorage, Alaska, 1982." Can you tell me anything about this card?

It is of questionable legitimacy. It was issued in 1987, not 1982, although it does purport to be an official team issue. It will never have much collector value since it was not issued when he was actually playing in the Alaska amateur league.

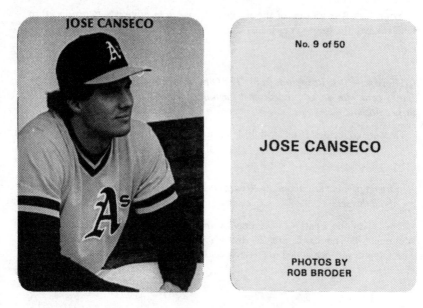

I have a card (#9) of Jose Canseco. It's in color. The back is white and says "Photos by Rob Broder." What type of card is this?

It's a collectors' issue, produced for the collector market rather than as a premium with another product, such as bubble gum. The Broder cards were not authorized by the players or teams.

I bought a pack of eight old-timers' cards at a supermarket. They were issued in 1981 by Cramer Sports Promotions. How much are these worth? Are they popular with collectors?

These are a collectors' issue, which were also re-issued in wax packs in various parts of the country. They are worth exactly what you paid for them, since these types of cards almost never attain any premium value.

I recently purchased a 100-card package of baseball cards. In it were eight different Willie Mays cards, each having red borders with stars in the corners. The backs form part of a puzzle. Can you identify these cards for me?

The eight cards you have are a part of a 90-card set produced by Renata Galasso in 1984. The set is a collectors' issue and highlights Mays' career. The card backs form a puzzle featuring 40 of Mays' Topps and Bowman cards.

Reprints, Collectors' Issues & Counterfeits

I have a black-and-white Ted Williams card (#230). It says "Ted Williams Hits .406" on the front, and on the back is a note that says it is from a sixth series from Renata Galasso, 1984. Can you identify this card and give its value?

Your card is from one of the dozens of collectors edition sets produced by Galasso over the years. They have no collector value.

I have three Pete Rose cards from "The Official Pete Rose Card Set" and an Ernie Banks card with an ad printed on it for hobby dealer Renata Galasso. What are these cards and their value?

They are collectors' issues with little or no value.

A friend of mine has about 30-40 cards titled "Famous Feats." What can you tell me about this set?

The "Famous Feats" set is one of many produced by artist Robert G. McLaughlin. The cards are 2½" by 3½", and feature cartoon drawings. All McLaughlin sets are collectors' issues, and generate practically no hobby interest.

I have a set called "The Mickey Mantle Story." I rarely see it at card shows or in card shops. It's not even listed or mentioned in any price guides. Why?

Because it's a recent collectors' issue.

I bought an 11-card set (10 rookies and Jose Canseco, the first 40/40 man). The set has two Jefferies, two Graces, and one Sabo, Jordan, Weiss, Griffey Jr., and Kelly. They look like snapshots, with no border and no stats on the back. They have rounded corners. The back has a cartoon-like picture of a man sliding. It says, "1989 Rookies I . . . #". Who made this set and what is its approximate value?

We could tell you who puts this out, but we don't like to publicize these illegal card sets. This is one of several privately issued "pirate" sets; they pay no royalties to the teams or players. They are, for all intents and purposes, worthless. Collectors must learn to discriminate between real baseball cards and the unlicensed junk.

I have a Gregg Jefferies card with orange letters saying "All Star" and his picture in front of a large red star. It was made by Pacific Cards & Comics of Los Angeles, #8 of 12. I can't find it listed anywhere. Please comment on this.

It's an unlicensed, unauthorized issue. It has no collector value.

Some time ago, I bought a card of Dwight Gooden. It's black-and-white and shows him wearing a warm-up jacket and holding his glove in front of him. The back has card #1 and a biography and 1984 stats. Can you tell me what set this card came from?

It probably wasn't part of any set. It appears to be an unauthorized collectors' issue. As such, it has no legitimate value.

Counterfeits

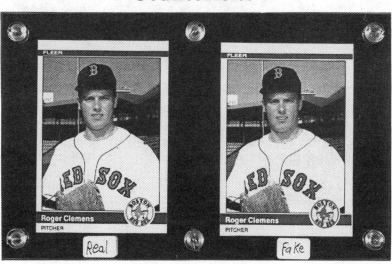

What can you tell me about counterfeit cards?

In recent years, more than 30 superstar cards from the 1960s-1980s have been counterfeited. All were quickly detected because of the differences in the quality of cardboard on which they were printed as well as the printing quality of the cards. A collector's best defense against counterfeits is to acquire a knowledge of the "look" and "feel" of genuine baseball cards of various eras and issues. Also, comparing a known original card to a suspected forgery can yield telltale differences. Krause Publications has published a book, the *Sports Collectors Digest Sportscard Counterfeit Detector,* which desribes and defines how to detect counterfeit cards.

I recently paid $10 at a show for a card that appeared to be a Mint 1963 Topps Pete Rose rookie card. Upon further examination, I discovered the back had been stamped "Counterfeit" and "Original Reprint." The seller was unsure of the card's history. What is the story behind this counterfeiting? How many exist? Is it considered an appreciating collectible? Do any other such cards exist?

Back in early 1982, a Los Angeles area printer was paid to produce 10,000

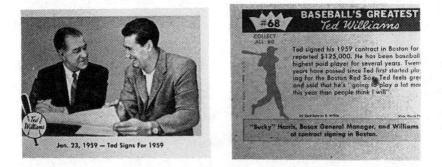

BASEBALL'S GREATEST
Ted Williams
#68
COLLECT ALL 80

Ted signed his 1959 contract in Boston for reported $125,000. He has been baseball's highest paid player for several years. Twenty years have passed since Ted first started playing for the Boston Red Sox. Ted feels great and said that he's "going to play a lot more this year than people think I will".

"Bucky" Harris, Bosox General Manager, and Williams at contract signing in Boston.

Jan. 23, 1959 — Ted Signs For 1959

counterfeit Rose rookie cards. The fakes were quickly spotted and a California dealer, Sheldon Jaffee, who police described as the "mastermind" of the plot, was convicted on related charges.

A large number of the fake cards were sold to hobby dealers after the trial with the stipulation that they be marked as counterfeits. The cards initially sold for as much as $20, and have been drifting downward in price ever since. They cannot be considered to be a collectible with any future potential for appreciation.

A similar situation exists with a quantity of card #68, which was withdrawn from the 1959 Fleer Ted Williams set. It was later illegally reprinted and can be found with a reprint notation on its back.

I have a complete set of six Babe Ruth cards from the 1928 Fro-Joy set I got at a flea market in 1983. The cards are printed on dark blue on white (except for some slight yellowing by age) and measure 2½" by 4½". The price guide books describe the set as black-and-white, and measuring 2⅟₁₆" by 4". I have heard of a reprint set, but I am sure my cards are authentic. Do you know of any variations in this set that would explain the difference between my cards and the price guides' descriptions?

We don't know why you're so sure your cards are real — we'll bet the person who sold them to you told you they were. Your description matches perfectly recent fakes. There are many ways to artificially "age" paper or cardboard, so the yellowing is no real proof of originality.

I have the 1975 TCMA International League set. Your catalog says there is a counterfeit being sold. How can I tell if mine is original?

The original set is printed on porous off-white paper. The reprint is on a hard white paper.

Do you know if the minor league cards TCMA put into assortment packs are real or counterfeit? I have cards Kirk McCaskill and Ivan Calderon. How do you go about pricing these singles?

The minor league cards found in those assortment packs are unauthorized reprints of original TCMA issues. They can be identified by the major league logo on the back. They have no collector value. Because of the ease with which minor league cards can be reprinted, we caution against buying singles of star players.

I bought a 1980 Greensboro Hornets minor league card of Don Mattingly. I can't find the set listed in any price guide. Why?

Because it's a fake. The card is a fantasy issue. There was no 1980 Greensboro card of Mattingly. It was printed in the last few years to dupe the unsuspecting.

I have a 1984 Donruss Don Mattingly rookie card. While comparing it to another Donruss card from that year's set, I noticed that the cardboard of the Mattingly card is more flexible. Also, the card is a little blurry at the bottom right where it says "Donruss '84." The type on the back seems to be thinner than the card used for comparison. Do I have a counterfeit Mattingly?

It sure sounds like you do. It was reported that a 14-year-old boy convinced a printer to produce 1,000 of the fake Mattingly Donruss rookies. The fakes first surfaced at a show in Fort Lauderdale, Fla., in late 1986. The boy was later apprehended and forced to make restitution. Perhaps the greatest telltale sign of the fakes is the thin glossy stock.

Reprints, Collectors' Issues & Counterfeits

I have two cards, one of Darryl Strawberry and one of Don Mattingly, that are 1984 Topps Nestle cards, except they are black-and-white. I can't seem to find out what they are, how rare they are or what they are worth.

They are counterfeits. They are as common as dirt and worth about as much.

Can you give me some information on a minor league card I recently obtained? It is a Ken Griffey Jr. San Bernadino Spirit card with dark blue borders and "San Bernadino" and "Spirit" written down the sides of the card. The back is quite plain, with no company or copyright stated. It has all his biographical data and 1987 Bellingham stats. In the corner is a large number 34 in a gray box. Is this card a fake? If not, what's its value? What company made it?

The card is an illegal rip-off of Cal Cards' genuine Spirit card set of 1988. Unless you buy the complete team set, you're possibly getting a counterfeit of the Griffey card. The fakes are worthless.

I recently bought a Will Clark 1984 U.S.A. Baseball Team card. It looks exactly the same as the 1985 Topps Mark McGwire card except for the back, which gives general information and says "Official U.S.A. Olympic Sponsor Card." Is this a 1984 issue? Could it be considered his minor league rookie? Does the card have any future value potential?

You've been stuck with a modern (1989 or so) fantasy card. It's unlicensed and unauthorized. It has no future value potential because whoever printed them first wouldn't hesistate to reprint them in the unlikely event the value ever started to rise.

I have a black-and-white Michael Jordan card. On the front it has him in a White Sox uniform swinging a bat. On the bottom it says "Air Knows." On the back it has "Air Jordan." It doesn't have any year or brand name. What kind of card is it? What is it worth?

It's an illegal, unlicensed card. It's junk and has no collector value.

Collecting Autographs

Chapter Nine

I heard about sending a baseball card in the mail and getting it autographed. Could you give me information on this and the address to send the card to?

Some players will autograph requests by mail. It's best to wait for the baseball season to start, then send your request in care of the team's stadium address. (Addresses for Major League Baseball, National Football League, National Hockey League and National Basketball Association teams are listed at the end of this section).

Here's a few key rules for autograph collectors: Always write a short, sincere note requesting the autograph, and the reason why you want the autograph. Never send more than two or three items to be signed. You can ask if the player can include a postcard or photo. Always send a self-addressed stamped envelope to return your card to you. Never send a ball or anything bulky. And lastly, don't waste your time or money sending to most baseball superstars — they receive too much fan mail to answer it all. We have found superstars from the NBA, on the other hand, to be very cooperative via the mail.

If I send a player a baseball card to autograph, is he obligated to sign it?

Not only is the player not obligated to sign it, he's not obligated to return it! A word of warning: Never send any card you don't want to risk permanently losing. Many of the biggest name stars receive too much fan mail to answer it all.

I'm interested in obtaining autographs of retired players. Should the letter be addressed to the player's home address or a team for which he played?

We suggest you purchase a copy of the *Sport Americana Baseball Address List* by Jack Smalling. It contains the home addresses of thousands of current and retired players. We recommend not sending autograph requests to a current player's home address; many refuse to sign items sent to their home. For current players, we recommend sending autograph requests to the stadium.

Collecting Autographs

Is there a list of players who sign and don't sign through the mail?

No such list exists. However, *Baseball Cards, Card News* and *Sports Collectors Digest* writer Dave Miedema frequently writes about players who are cooperative and those who are not.

What are the rules as far as getting an autograph from a player in person?

The ballpark is fine. When a player is eating dinner with his family at a restaurant, that's not fine. The hotel or airport is OK. The player's home is not OK. Use good judgement when approaching a player for an autograph. Be courteous and address him by his first name or by Mr. (last name). He will be more apt to sign for you if you say "Eric" or "Mr. Davis," rather than "Hey you, Davis." Don't ask a player to sign more than two or three items (many players limit the number of in-person autographs to one). And remember that players, like all of us, have bad days (and bad games), and sometimes will not honor your autograph request.

I recently purchased an official National League baseball and would like to have it autographed by Nolan Ryan, Rollie Fingers, Tom Seaver and Steve Carlton. How do I go about it?

The best way is to attend card shows where these players are autograph guests. An alternative is to send the ball to shows, if the promoters advertise that they accept mail-order autograph sales. Forget sending balls to a player's home or team; most do not want to be bothered with the hassle of packaging and mailing balls.

How do I get signatures of players from Canadian teams?

When writing any Canadian club, you'll have to enclose a self-addressed stamped envelope, with a Canadian stamp on the SASE. Don't send money and expect the player to buy stamps for you. Check a local stamp shop for Canadian stamps.

Collecting Autographs

Can you tell me what it means when an autographed baseball is signed on the "manager's spot?"

The "manager's spot" or "sweet spot" is the premium location on the ball; it is the large blank horizontal area between the seams and opposite the league president's imprinted name. The name comes from team-signed balls, on which this spot was customarily left blank for the skipper's signature as a sign of respect.

I have noticed on many autographs I have obtained, players write "Rom" and a time, such as "Rom 10:17." What does "Rom" stand for?

It's not a time — it's a Biblical reference. "Rom" is the New Testament Epistle of Paul the Apostle to the Romans. The number on the left of the colon refers to the chapter, and the right-hand number refers to a specific verse which has a meaning to the player. Some players sign their autographs this way as a means of attesting to their Christian faith.

I am told some players refuse to sign Topps cards, but will sign other cards. Why is this?

Several major leaguers, including Glenn Davis of the Baltimore Orioles, have boycotted signing Topps cards to demonstrate their opposition to Topps' Garbage Pail Kids cards. Some players refuse to sign cards that depict them with a certain team (regardless of the maker), while others may not sign at all because they are afraid the item they sign will be resold. A few players will sign only when an autograph request is accompanied by a check to their charity.

I read that Sharpie pens are no good for autographs on a baseball. I have a great many valuable autographs on baseballs. Most were signed with a black Sharpie pen. Please tell me how to preserve these autographs. What kind of pen should I use on a baseball?

The problem with Sharpie-signed autographs, which makes them great for signing glossy photographs and baseball cards, makes them bad for signing baseballs. Sharpie ink bleeds into the cover of a baseball, making a fat signature fatter and more illegible. And the ink continues to deteriorate, eventually making the signature totally illegible. Nothing really stops the deterioration, although you might try spraying the ball with a coat or two of artist's fixative.

Balls should be signed with a ball-point pen with an even ink flow. If you're at a card show, want to have a ball signed, and aren't certain if they'll have a good ball-point pen at the autograph table, bring along one of your own.

What type of ink/pen should be used for players to sign on cards? I have been using a regular black pen, but I have seen some folks using large — but sharp pointed — indelible marking pens for signatures.

211

Collecting Autographs

The preferred pen to get cards signed is by the felt-tip "Sharpie" that you describe. Blue is the most popular color. Be careful though, when having glossy cards or photos signed, not to handle them or put them into a plastic sheet until the ink has thoroughly dried to prevent smearing.

I see many people at shows getting bats autographed. What kind of pen is used that won't smudge?

Sharpie brand felt-tip pens are usually used for signing bats. If left alone for a couple of minutes after signing, they will not smudge on the bat's surface.

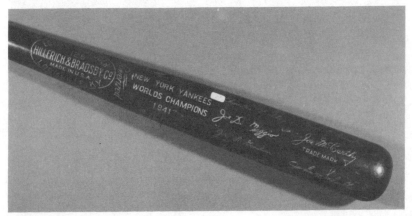

I am an avid collector of autographed baseballs. Besides the plastic ball holder, which is the best way to preserve these from fading, smears, etc.?

Frankly, there is no better way to preserve or display autographed balls than the several types of plastic holders now on the market. We especially like the kind which pairs a card holder on a wooden base, so that a card or photo can be displayed along with the ball. There are some spray fixatives available at art supply stores that can be used to prevent smearing or smudging signatures, but they may cause the ink to run if improperly applied. To prevent fading, keep balls out of direct sunlight, and, as much as possible, away from indoor lighting.

Collecting Autographs

I recently purchased a Spalding official All-Star ball with many signatures, including Nolan Ryan, Joe Torre, Tom Seaver and Bob Gibson. The signatures are all stamped on. Any guesses where the ball came from? I paid $20 for it — did I get ripped off?

The key word here is "stamped." Balls which have the "autographs" machine-printed on them in this manner have no collector value. Such mass-produced souvenirs are usually sold in the concession stands at the All-Star Game.

How can I tell the difference between a real autograph and a fake one when buying through the mail?

It's very difficult. Unless you see an autograph being signed with your own eyes, you never know for sure. There's no substitute for experience in viewing samples of player signatures, but even the experts can be fooled. When buying an autograph, you have to rely on the honesty of the seller.

Generally, a person who has been dealing in autographs for a long period of time has probably acquired the expertise to know good from bad and to avoid passing along fakes to his customers. A dishonest autograph dealer usually becomes the object of numerous customer complaints and is quickly driven out of the pages of honest hobby publications.

What is ghost-signing? How can you tell the difference between authentic and ghost-signed autographs?

Ghost-signing means somebody else actually signed the autograph. In the real world, this is known as forgery. Many popular players, from Babe Ruth to today's stars, have resorted to having the clubhouse boy, a rookie teammate, or a family member sign autographs for them. The way to know for sure if an auto-graph is authentic is to see it signed in person. Careful comparison between a suspect autograph and a known authentic signature may reveal significant differ-ences which would lead to the conclusion that it is ghosted.

I was told that some players use an "auto-pen" or "rubber stamp" to sign cards. Could you explain what they are, and what effect they have on the price of a card?

An auto-pen is a machine which mechanically duplicates a player's signature. While the machine's programming is based on his signature, it is not actually signed by him. A rubber stamp is a stamp that contains the player's signature and is stamped on a card. As to the value, collectors view an auto-pen or rubber-stamped item to be defaced, thus selling for about the value of a Fair card.

I have an Upper Deck 1990 Reggie Jackson personally-autographed card. Some dealers have told me it is worth $1. Others have told me it is worth $1,000. Please tell me the real price.

First you have to know if you have one of the real genuinely-autographed Jackson cards. All of the cards carry a facsimile autograph, but the 2,500 ones with the real Reggie signature have a diamond-shaped hologram on the back, rather than the circle. A genuine Reggie-signed Upper Deck prize card retails in the $600-750 range.

215

Collecting Autographs

A while ago, I received an autographed ball of Ted Williams and Yogi Berra from my priest. The ball is a "Ted Williams Autograph League Ball" made by Wilson. I was told this ball isn't going to be worth anything because it isn't an official American or National League ball. Is that true?

As a rule, autographed balls are worth more signed on an official league ball than on a non-official ball. That doesn't mean, however, your ball is worthless.

Is there some sort of magic formula that says a card's or ball's value increases by some percentage if it is signed?

There is no set figure by which a player's autograph increases the value of a card or ball (or any other item). Common sense would give you a ballpark figure by adding the value of the card (or other item) to the value of the player's autograph. The player's autograph value can be determined by the current price of an autograph ticket at the shows he does.

Other advice: refrain from having older and more valuable cards in top-notch condition signed. Use off-condition cards for that purpose. In most instances, newer star cards with autographs are worth more. However, that does not hold true for high-priced star cards, such as Don Mattingly rookie.

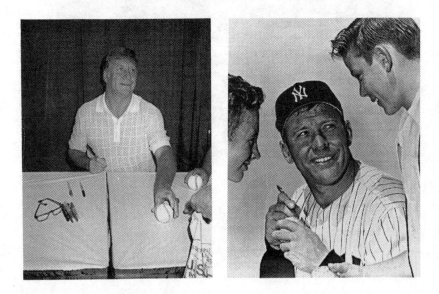

I have a baseball signed by Mickey Mantle, but it is addressed to a police officer whose nickname is "Bullet." How much is his signature worth, and do the other words take the value down?

216

Currently, anyone with $5 for a baseball and $25 or so for a Mantle autograph ticket can get an autographed ball during Mantle's many card show autograph appearances. This effectively sets the worth of a Mantle-autographed ball. The personalization does make the ball harder to sell (unless you know somebody nicknamed "Bullet"), and thus worth less than a ball with just Mantle's autograph.

I got my 1980 Topps Rickey Henderson rookie card autographed at a show. Some dealers say this decreased the price of the card. Is it true?

Not technically. Theoretically, the value of an autographed card increases in direct proportion to the popularity of the player. However, what really happened is the autograph greatly reduces the number of potential buyers. When you do find a buyer, he will likely pay more for the card with the autograph — if you can convince him that it's genuine.

I attended the game Don Sutton won his 300th career victory. After the game, I acquired his autograph on a ticket stub. Later I had it laminated. Did this ruin the possible collector value?

In general, laminating a non-card collectible does not so much ruin its collector value as it limits the number of potential buyers. Laminating an autograph item is always risky because of the potential that the glue on the lamination could react unfavorably to the type of ink with which the autograph was signed.

In 1963, I went to Cooperstown with an All-Star Babe Ruth team from Ottawa, Ontario, Canada. While there, I received a gift of an official Babe Ruth league baseball autographed by Mrs. Babe Ruth. Would you be able to hazard a guess as to its value.

An interesting collectible, but not one with a great amount of value. We would place it in the $25-$50 range. You can contact autograph dealers who may state otherwise.

I have a baseball autographed by the 1929 Philadelphia Athletics championship team. Included are the signatures of Jimmie Foxx, Mickey Cochrane, Lefty Grove and others. Can you tell me what it's worth and how I can sell it?

Depending on its condition, you could realize more than $500 for the ball if you decided to part with it. As for selling it, your best bet is to get a copy of *Sports Collectors Digest,* a weekly magazine that features many ads for rare and valuable sports collectibles.

Major League Baseball

Baltimore Orioles — Memorial Stadium, Baltimore, Md. 21218.

Boston Red Sox — Fenway Park, 4 Yawkey Way, Boston, Mass. 02215.

California Angels — Anaheim Stadium, 2000 State College Blvd., Anaheim, Calif. 92806.

Chicago White Sox — Comiskey Park, 333 W. 35th St., Chicago, Ill. 60616.

Cleveland Indians — Cleveland Stadium, Boudreau Blvd., Cleveland, Ohio 44114.

Detroit Tigers — Tiger Stadium, Detroit, Mich. 48216.

Kansas City Royals — P.O. Box 419969, Kansas City, Mo. 64141.

Milwaukee Brewers — County Stadium, Milwaukee, Wis. 53214.

Minnesota Twins — HHH Metrodome, 501 Chicago Ave. S., Minneapolis, Minn. 55415.

New York Yankees — Yankee Stadium, Bronx, N.Y. 10451.

Oakland A's —Oakland Coliseum, Oakland, Calif. 94621.

Seattle Mariners — 110 S. King St., Seattle, Wash. 98104.

Texas Rangers — P.O. Box 1111, Arlington, Texas 76010.

Toronto Blue Jays — The SkyDome, 300 The Esplanade West, Suite #3200, Toronto, Ontario, Canada M5V 3B3.

Atlanta Braves — P.O. Box 4064, Atlanta, Ga. 30302.

Chicago Cubs — Clark & Addison Sts., Chicago, Ill. 60613.

Cincinnati Reds — 100 Riverfront Stadium, Cincinnati, Ohio 45202.

Houston Astros — P.O. Box 288, Houston, Texas 77001.

Los Angeles Dodgers — 1000 Elysian Park Avenue, Los Angeles, Calif. 90012.

Montreal Expos — P.O. Box 500, Station M, Montreal, Quebec, Canada H1V 3P2.

New York Mets — 126th St. & Roosevelt Ave., Flushing, N.Y. 11368.

Philadelphia Phillies — P.O. Box 7575, Philadelphia, Pa. 19101.

Pittsburgh Pirates — 600 Stadium Circle, Pittsburgh, Pa. 15212.

St. Louis Cardinals — 250 Stadium Plaza, St. Louis, Mo. 63102.

San Diego Padres — P.O. Box 2000, San Diego, Calif. 92120.

San Francisco Giants — Candlestick Park, San Franscico, Calif. 94124.

National Basketball Association

Atlanta Hawks — One CNN Center, South Tower, Suite 405, Atlanta, Ga. 30303.

Boston Celtics — 150 Causeway St., Boston, Mass. 02114.

Charlotte Hornets — Two First Union Plaza, Suite 2600, Charlotte, N.C. 28282.

Chicago Bulls — One Magnificent Mile, 980 North Michigan Ave., Suite 1600, Chicago, Ill. 60611.

Cleveland Cavaliers — P.O. Box 5000, Richfield, Ohio 44286-5000.

Dallas Mavericks — Reunion Arena, 777 Sports Street, Dallas, Texas 75207.

Denver Nuggets — P.O. Box 4658, Denver, Colo. 80204-0658.

Detroit Pistons — The Palace of Auburn Hills, One Championship Drive, Auburn Hills, Mich. 48057.

Golden State Warriors — Oakland Coliseum Arena, Nimitz Freeway & Hegenberger Road, Oakland, Calif. 94621.

Houston Rockets — P.O. Box 272349, Houston, Texas 77277.

Indiana Pacers — 300 East Market Street, Indianapolis, Ind. 46204.

Los Angeles Clippers — Los Angeles Sports Arena, 3939 South Figueroa, Los Angeles, Calif. 90037.

Los Angeles Lakers — P.O. Box 10, Inglewood, Calif. 90306.

Miami Heat — Miami Arena, Miami, Fla. 33136-4102.

Milwaukee Bucks — The Bradley Center, 1001 North Fourth St., Milwaukee, Wis. 53203.

Minnesota Timberwolves — 500 City Place, 730 Hennepin Ave., Suite 500, Minneapolis, Minn. 55403.

New Jersey Nets — Brendan Byrne Arena, East Rutherford, N.J. 07073.

New York Knicks — 4 Pennsylvania Plaza, New York, NY 10001

Orlando Magic — Orlando Arena, One Magic Place, Orlando, Fla. 32801.

Philadelphia 76ers — The Spectrum, Philadelphia, Pa. 19148.

Phoenix Suns — P.O. Box 1369, Phoenix, Ariz. 85001.

Portland Trail Blazers — 700 NE Multnomah St., Suite 950-Lloyd Building, Portland, Ore. 97232.

Sacramento Kings — One Sports Parkway, Sacramento, Calif. 95834.

San Antonio Spurs — 600 East Market, Suite 102, San Antonio, Texas 78205.

Seattle Supersonics — Box C-900911, Seattle, Wash. 98109-9711.

Utah Jazz — 5 Traid Center, 5th Floor, Salt Lake City, Utah 84180.

Washington Bullets — Capital Centre, One Harry S. Truman Drive, Landover, Md. 20785.

National Hockey League

Boston Bruins — Boston Gardens, Boston, Mass. 02114.

Buffalo Sabres — 140 Main St., Buffalo, N.Y. 14202.

Calgary Flames — P.O. Box 1540, Station "M", Calgary, Alberta, Canada T2P 3B9.

Chicago Blackhawks — 1800 W. Madison St., Chicago, Ill. 60612.

Detroit Red Wings — 600 Civic Center Drive, Detroit, Mich. 48226.

Edmonton Oilers — 7424 118th Ave., Edmonton, Alberta, Canada T5B 4M9.

Hartford Whalers — One Civic Center Drive, Hartford, Conn. 06103.

Los Angeles Kings — The Forum, Inglewood, Calif. 90306.

Minnesota Northstars — 7901 Clear Ave. S., Bloomington, Minn. 55420.

Montreal Canadiens — The Forum, Montreal, Quebec, Canada H3H 1N2.

New Jersey Devils — Meadowlands Arena, P.O. Box 504, E. Rutherford, N.J. 07073.

New York Islanders — Nassau Veterans Memorial Coliseum, Uniondale, N.Y. 11553.

Collecting Autographs

New York Rangers — 4 Pennsylvania Plaza, New York, N.Y. 10001.
Philadelphia Flyers — The Spectrum, Philadelphia, Pa. 19148.
Pittsburgh Penguins — Civic Arena, Gate #7, Pittsburgh, Pa. 15219.
Quebec Nordiques — 2205 Ave. Du Colissee, Quebec City, PQ, Canada G1L 4W7.
St. Louis Blues — 5700 Oakland Ave., St. Louis, Mo. 63110.
Toronto Maple Leafs — 60 Carlton St., Toronto, Ontario, Canada M6B L1L.
Vancouver Canucks — 100 N. Renfrew Street, Vancouver, B.C., Canada V5K 3N7
Washington Capitals — Capital Centre, Landover, Md. 20786.
Winnipeg Jets — 15-1430 Maroons Road, Winnipeg, Manitoba, Canada R3G OL5.

National Football League

Atlanta Falcons — I-85 and Suwanee Road, Suwanee, Ga. 30174.
Buffalo Bills — One Bills Drive, Orchard Park, N.Y. 14127.
Chicago Bears — 250 N. Washington, Lake Forest, Ill. 60045.
Cincinnati Bengals — 200 Riverfront Stadium, Cincinnati, Ohio 45202.
Cleveland Browns — Tower B, Cleveland Stadium, Cleveland, Ohio 44114.
Dallas Cowboys — One Cowboys Parkway, Irving, Texas 75063.
Denver Broncos — 5700 Logan St., Denver, Colo. 80216.
Detroit Lions — Pontiac Silverdome, 1200 Featherstone Road, Pontiac, Mich. 48057.
Green Bay Packers — 1265 Lombardi Drive, Green Bay, Wis. 54307.
Houston Oilers — 6910 Fannin St., Houston, Texas 77030.
Indianapolis Colts — 7001 W. 56th St., Indianapolis, Ind. 46254.
Kansas City Chiefs — Arrowhead Stadium, Kansas City, Mo. 64129.
Los Angeles Raiders — 332 Center St., El Segundo, Calif. 90245.
Los Angeles Rams — 2327 W. Lincoln Ave., Anaheim, Calif. 92801.
Miami Dolphins — 2269 NW 199th St., Miami, Fla. 33056.
Minnesota Vikings — 9520 Vikings Drive, Eden Prairie, Minn. 55344.
New England Patriots — Sullivan Stadium, Route 1, Foxboro, Mass. 02035.
New Orleans Saints — 1500 Paydras St., New Orleans, La. 70112.
New York Giants — Giants Stadium, E. Rutherford, N.J. 07073
New York Jets — 598 Madison Ave., New York, N.Y. 10022.
Philadelphia Eagles — Veterans Stadium, Broad Street and Pattison Avenue, Philadelphia, Pa. 19148.
Phoenix Cardinals — P.O. Box 888, Phoenix, Ariz. 85001-0888.
Pittsburgh Steelers — 300 Stadium Circle, Pittsburgh, Pa. 15212.
San Diego Chargers — Jack Murphy Stadium, San Diego, Calif. 92120.
San Francisco 49ers — 4949 Centennial Blvd., Santa Clara, Calif. 95954.
Seattle Seahawks — 11220 NE 5 3rd St., Kirkland, Wash. 98033.
Tampa Bay Buccaneers — One Buccaneer Place, Tampa, Fla. 33607.
Washington Redskins — Dulles International Airport, P.O. Box 17247, Washington, D.C. 20041.

Baseball
Memorabilia

Chapter Ten

Baseball Coins

I have discovered some plastic Salada Tea and Junket Brand Dessert baseball coins. I think they are from the 1960s. Can you tell me about them?

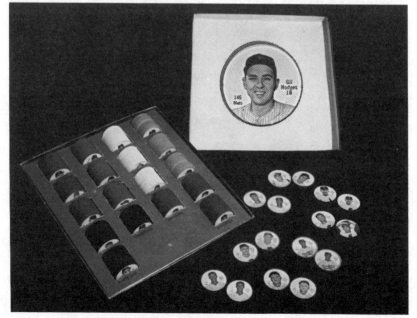

Baseball Memorabilia

Check them out in the *Standard Catalog of Baseball Cards.* Plastic Salada coins were issued in 1962. There were 221 different players issued, with 40 variations in the set. Some of the rare variations sell for more than $1,000. Common coins are $2 in decent condition. Salada also had a 63-piece metal coin set the following year.

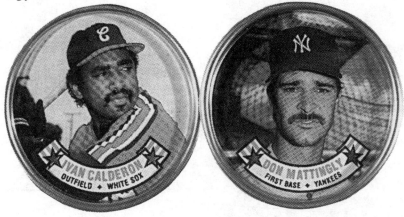

I recently purchased some 1988 Topps baseball coins. Are they worth collecting?

The 60 metal discs which make up the 1988 Topps coin set measure $1\frac{1}{2}$" in diameter. We think they're a neat item and certainly worth collecting for their uniqueness alone.

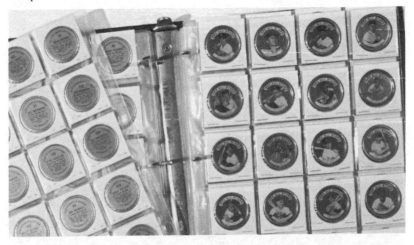

I have a Willie Mays coin that says "1964 All-Stars" on the front. On the back, it has #151. On the bottom it says, "Collect all 44 special All-Stars." Who made this set?

That's from the Topps 1964 wax pack insert set of 164 coins. There were 44 special All-Star coins in the set and 120 regular player coins (see above). The set is $650 in Near Mint condition; your Mays AS coin is an $18 item.

I have some metal discs I believe were made in 1971. They have a player photo on the front and a short biography on the back. What are these discs?

The metal "coins" you own are part of a 153-piece set produced by Topps in 1971. The coins, measuring 1½" in diameter, were inserts in packs of Topps cards. A complete set of coins in Near Mint condition has a value of $400.

I found five plastic discs. Two of them are Bob Skinner, one is Bob Cerv and two are Jackie Jensen. One of them is green, another red, and the other three are orange.

On the back they tell the player's batting average. Can you tell me more about them?

You've got examples from the second of three Armour Franks "coin" sets. The hot dog company issued them in packages of weiners in 1955, 1959 and 1960. There were 24 players in the 1955 set, and 20 each in the 1959 and 1960 sets. Advanced collectors sometimes chase these by color variation; the same players are sometimes found on different colored plastic.

We've heard of one particularly scarce 1960 Armour coin, Bud Daley, recently selling for several hundred dollars. Also of note is a $375 1955 Mickey Mantle coin with his name spelled correctly. An error Mantle coin exists with his name spelled "Mantel," valued at $120. Depending on the year, Armour coins of common players sell for around $5-$10, with Hall of Famers bringing as much as $18-$35.

My mother was going through some old stuff and gave me a 1969 Pete Rose Baseball Centennial Series coin. Can you tell me anything about it?

This is from a 20-piece (10 National League, 10 American League) Citgo gas station giveaway issue from 1969. A display board also exists for the set. The Rose coin is the most valuable, worth up to $20.

I cannot locate or identify the origin of a 12-coin set of St. Louis Cardinals "Busch Stadium Immortals 1909-1966." They are gold colored and are mounted in a cardboard display that stands upright. Do you know anything about this or if any other such sets were produced for the Cardinals or other teams?

The set was produced to mark the May 12, 1966, move out of old Busch Stadium (formerly Sportsman's Park) into the Cardinals current riverfront stadium. The first 11 home games of 1966 were played at old Busch Stadium. The team gave away the holder and the medals to fans attending those games, which honored the players pictured on the medals.

Complete sets of these gold-toned aluminum medals were sold by the team to collectors for $7 each, with individual medals available for 50 cents. We don't know of any similar sets of medals, although there have been dozens of individual player medals produced over the years.

Pins & Buttons

I have about 10 really small 1969 pins. There is nothing on the back, but on the sides in small print it says "1969 MLBPA MFG IN USA." I have players such as Brooks Robinson, Ted Williams, Joe DiMaggio, Al Kaline, Satchel Paige, Don Drysdale, Whitey Ford and Sandy Koufax. Are they worth anything?

No, because they are a recent (mid-1980s) fantasy collectors' issue patterned after the genuine 60-pin 1969 Major League Baseball Players Association issue, which featured only then-current players.

I recently purchased a 1910 P2 pin of Ty Cobb. Could you please give some general information about the P2 pins?

We assume you're referring to the Sweet Caporal pins, which were given away with cigarettes between 1910-1912. A total of 152 pins are known, plus variations. Most of the variations have the player's name in larger letters. The Ty Cobb pin has a large-letter variation. In top grades, the Cobb pin has a catalog value of $200, while the large-letter variation goes for $325.

My great-great uncle gave me a pin that I know nothing about. It's bronzelike in color, and in the shape of a baseball bat, about 1½" long, with a baseball behind it. Written across the bat are the words "Dizzy Dean Winners." I would appreciate any information you could give me about this old pin.

Your pin is one of five different prizes that could be found in boxes of Post Grape Nuts cereal in the 1930s, all related to Dizzy Dean. There was a badge, a couple of rings, a token and your pin. Value is in the $15-$30 range.

In my collection are pin-back buttons produced by Crane Potato Chips in the 1960s. Are these pins popular with collectors?

The team logo pins you have were part of a baseball contest sponsored by Crane Potato Chips each year from 1961 to 1969. Some years are noted on the pin backs; other years are not. Because they do not feature players, the pins have generated very little collector interest. Pin value ranges from 50 cents to $2.

Baseball Memorabilia

I have two large buttons which commemorate the day Mickey Mantle retired. One has white letters, one has black letters. Could you please tell me how many variations were printed and how they were distributed to the public?

The large buttons were sold inside and outside the stadium, on Mantle's official retirement day and afterwards. No other letter variations are known.

In 1985, Fun Food Co. made a set of 133 buttons with star baseball players on them. I bought a set because I thought they would be very rare in a few years. Have they increased in value since they were made?

The Fun Food pins did get rare in a few years. The only thing rarer is somebody who wants to buy them. Value has remained about the same — $25 a set, or so.

I have a pin-back button of Willie Mays. It has a white background with his name in bold black type. A red, white and blue ribbon hangs down from the button. Can you give me any information on this?

Although we are not familiar with this particular button, we do know that buttons of this nature were sold at ballparks during the 1950s and 1960s.

I have quite a few 1956 Topps pins that I bought as a kid. Can you comment on them?

A limited-edition issue of 60 player pins was one of the first Topps specialty issues. The pictures are the same as found on regular Topps cards that year. The 1⅛ diameter pins include a lot of stars and three unaccountable rare pieces — Hecter Lopez, Chuck Diering and Chuck Stobbs, worth more than $175 each. The Hall of Famers in the set bring from $50-$100, with the complete set valued at $2,500 in Near Mint condition. The pins are really quite rare, and if they were at all popular with collectors would sell for a lot more money.

Baseball Games

I have a baseball game produced by Milton Bradley in 1970 which also includes a set of baseball cards to be used to play a game. Are these cards collectible?

Because the cards have black-and-white photos and no statistics, they are not overly popular with collectors. We've seen the complete game for sale anywhere from $50-$150. Our pricing experts agree $50 is a much more realistic figure.

I was cleaning out my closet recently and came across a Strat-o-matic baseball game with four complete teams, including the 1975 Reds and Red Sox, Yankees and Royals. Can I find cards of current players for the game?

Yes, Strat-o-matic continues to market new team sets of its round, pictureless player cards each year. The first was in 1961. There is some collector value in the older playing cards.

Recently I came across some cards — 37 in all, not a full deck — from a game called "The National Game." Each card has a picture of a different early-day ball-

player, along with the words "base hit," "foul ball," "strike," and so forth. What can you tell me about this set?

The set is called — naturally — "The National Game." It's a card game set, one of several issued in the 1910-1913 period. There are 44 cards in the set, so you're not far away from a complete set. The cards are worth about $25 each — more for Ty Cobb, Walter Johnson and Cy Young — depending on condition.

I purchased a game made by the Cincinnati Playing Card Co. called "Fan Craze." Can you provide me with some information about this game?

If you have the complete game with all the cards in the original box, then you have a nice piece of memorabilia. American League and National League versions of the Fan Craze game were produced in 1904. A complete set of 51 A.L. cards in Near Mint condition is valued at more than $1,000. The same goes for the N.L. set of 54 cards. Attach a premium to having the game box.

I have a 1957 Ed-U-Cards game. Is it worth keeping?

Is it worth keeping, as opposed to worth throwing way? Certainly. It's an enjoyable game to play, and although the cards have never really caught on as collectibles, that should not stop you from hanging onto it if you enjoy it. We've seen complete Ed-U-Card games advertised for $7 each.

Stamps & Envelopes

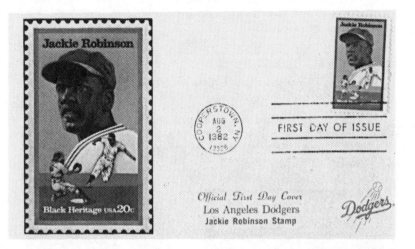

I bought some envelopes titled "First Day of Issue." They had pictures of Jackie Robinson and were made in Cooperstown, N.Y., Aug. 2, 1982. Please tell me more about these.

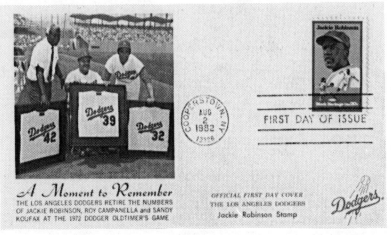

Baseball Memorabilia

There were many different styles of cacheted envelopes postmarked with the first day of issue cancellation when the Jackie Robinson stamp was issued in 1982. Some were produced in editions of hundreds or thousands, some were produced in very limited numbers. There is no catalog or checklist available of these items.

What is the best way to buy the Lou Gehrig stamps as a collectible investment? Individually or in sheets?

Don't buy the Gehrig stamps as an investment. With few exceptions, U.S. commemoratives have proven to have no investment value. If you want to gamble, buy the stamps in sheets.

I bought about three dozen paper stamp-like pictures. I asked several dealers about them, but no one can help me out. Do you know what they are?

Sure do. They're punched out from books published by Dell in the early 1970s. Books were issued for each team and had statistical information and a team schedule in addition to the punch-out photos. The punched-out photos are worth far less than the intact books.

Do Panini sticker albums actually become worth anything? Is it better to put the stickers in the album or leave the album blank?

Baseball player stamps and stickers have traditionally had very little collector value. While superstar collectors seek out those of the biggest-name players, there is no aftermarket for the sets or albums. Any value a set of modern stamps or stickers might develop will be higher if they are not glued into the album.

230

I have a 1955 Golden Stamp book of the Brooklyn Dodgers. Is it rare?

Not really. There was a large hoard of these books brought onto the market in the past couple of years. They are, however, quite expensive because of the enormous demand for Brooklyn Dodger collectibles. The book with stamp sheets intact (not pasted into the album) can bring $20-$50. There were also albums issued for the Milwaukee Braves, New York Giants and Cleveland Indians. These are much scarcer — especially the Indians — but don't bring any more money because of lower demand.

Baseball Books & Other Publications

What can you tell me about a small booklet, about 3¾" by 3", called the "1954 Edition Gillette World Series Record Book"?

It's one of a series of sports-related giveaways the razor blade company produced in the 1950s. They have a lot of good information in them, but no collector value.

I recently uncovered a set of booklets titled "Today's 1971 Los Angeles Dodgers," "Cincinnati Reds," etc., covering each of the 24 Major League teams in 1970. Each booklet has 24 color stamps, 2" by 3", of the team's players, plus stats from the 1970 season and earlier years. What do you know about these books? How many sets were produced? How were they sold? How many years did the set run, and do they have any value?

We've never seen any other year than 1971 for these booklets. They were marked at newsstands, etc., by Dell, one of the major magazine distributors. The booklet carries a 39-cent cover price, or a complete set of 24 could be ordered for $4.50. There's no telling how many were produced, but they remain fairly common even today, nearly 20 years later. They can be seen at card shows selling for $1-$2 for all but the most popular teams.

231

At a card store, I traded a 1972 Hank Aaron card for a Pete Rose booklet. On the front it says, "The Pete Rose Story." It is booklet No. 15 of 24. Did I get a deal? What year is it?

You probably came out about even on the deal. What you have is a 1970 Topps wax pack insert; Rose is the most valuable of the set, worth $8 in high grade. The complete set is valued around $25.

*I got a 1967 **Famous Slugger Yearbook** at an auction. It has 64 pages and measures 6½" by 4⅜". Can you supply any more information on it?*

Your Hillerich and Bradsby *Famous Slugger Yearbook* is one of several publications issued by the Louisville-based bat manufacturer. The yearbook was first issued in 1927 and is a cross between an informational publication and a catalog for Louisville Slugger bats. Your yearbook could be worth anywhere from $2-$5, depending on its condition.

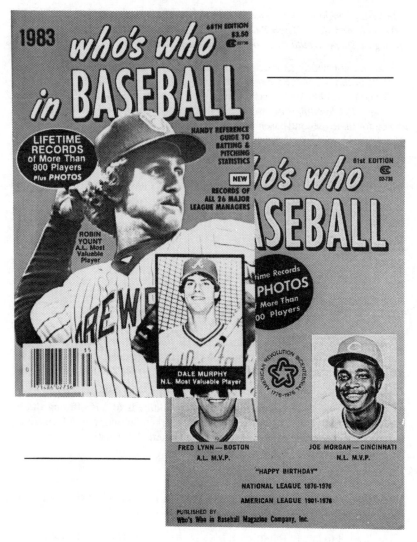

I have a book titled "Who's Who In The Major Leagues" from 1937. I cannot find any information as to what value this publication might have. Can you help?

The publication you have is valued in $40-$50 in top condition. Surprisingly, there is no current price guide for publications. Publications dealer B&E Collectibles (12 Marble Ave., Thornwood, N.Y. 10594) publishes a 50-page catalog that offers for sale older and newer sports publications. The catalog is available for $4 and should give you a good idea for what prices publications are currently selling.

233

Baseball Memorabilia

I recently bought a small collection of cards and books. Among the books was a 1907 "Lajoie's Official Baseball Guide." There's no cover on the book, but the pages are in great shape. Would it be worth anything to a memorabilia collector?

Yes, but not nearly as much as an example with a cover on it. Like cards, baseball books are valued largely on their condition. The Lajoie guides were published from 1906-1908 in competition with those from Spalding, *The Sporting News* and *The Sporting Life*. In decent shape with covers, the Lajoie guides — named for famed second baseman Napoleon Lajoie — can bring $50-$75.

I have a New York Yankees book from 1956 by Jay Publishing Co., with pictures of the 1955 World Series, player photos, bios, etc. Is it worth more or less than the "official" 1956 Yankees yearbook?

Less.

Scorecards & Yearbooks

Along with baseball cards, I collect scorecards, yearbooks, miniature bats, wrappers, ticket stubs and all sorts of sports-related nicknacks. Is there a publication you could recommend that would give me an idea on the value of items like that?

There is no specific price guide for such non-card collectibles, but if you scan the ads in *Sports Collectors Digest*, you'll find hundreds of ads offering these items. This will give you a feel for the current market. Subscription information for this magazine is available at the end of the General Information section.

I was given a 10-cent Cincinnati Reds scorebook from 1948. It has a picture of Bucky Walters on its front. Is this a program worth keeping?

Don't use it to line your bird cage. It's a swell collector's item. If in nice condition it is valued at $12-$15.

While going through my grandfather's basement, I found a 1963 scorecard for a Kansas City Athletics game against Baltimore. Does the writing inside decrease the value of the program?

Among specialists in programs, there is a difference of opinion as to whether the fact that the scorecard portion is actually used affects the value. Some prefer their program unscored, while others think a neatly and completely scored program is worth more because it provides a historical perspective of the game.

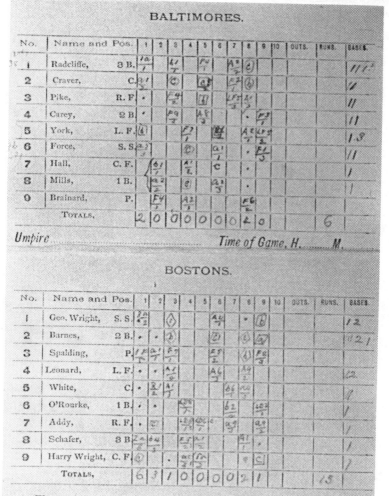

Unless the program in question is a World Series or All-Star program, a scored scorecard has little effect on the value today. A 1963 A's program in decent condition is a $5-$10 item, scored or not.

I have a 1984 Detroit Tigers scorebook and yearbook without rips or pencil marks. One friend says they are not worth anything, and one friend says they're worth saving. Who's right?

The friend who says to keep them. They're worth a couple of bucks each, and will go up in value in the future.

My dad was going through his old things and found a 1960 Chicago White Sox yearbook. Is it valuable?

It's worth about $15-$25, depending on condition (wear on spine, creases, torn pages, writing, tape marks and so forth). It's probably much more valuable than that to you and your father. The 1960 White Sox were a heck of a team.

I recently bought a 1986 New York Mets yearbook. Will it be worth anything in a couple of years?

Certainly. But probably not much more than what you paid for it. Modern yearbooks are produced — and more importantly, saved — in tremendous numbers. Large dealers are able to buy hundreds or thousands of books from some teams at year-end for a fraction of cover price. It is unlikely most recent yearbooks will see great value appreciation.

My dad has a 1978 Cincinnati Reds media fact book he got for $2.50. In this book, there are articles on all the Reds, including Vida Blue. The commissioner of baseball vetoed the trade from Oakland, so Blue never pitched for the Reds. Still, he's in the media guide. How much would this guide be worth now?

The fact Vida Blue is in the guide really doesn't have any impact on the value — less than $10 — of the guide; it's just interesting.

Baseball & Sports Magazines

*Do old magazines with baseball players on the cover have any value? I bought a 1961 **Life** magazine with Mantle and Maris on the cover for $4. Did I get a bargain?*

Yes, if the magazine is in nice condition. Collecting general circulation magazines, such as *Sport, Sports Illustrated, The Sporting News, Baseball Digest* and so forth, has become very popular in recent years. Values depend on the condition of the publication and who is depicted on the cover. Nice condition publications from the 1960s and 1970s may sell for $5-$15 if a popular player is on the cover.

*I have Vol. 1, No. 1, issue of **Sports Illustrated** in the original mailing cover with the baseball insert intact. The magazine is in excellent condition. Does the baseball card insert add to the value, or is the value based on it being the No. 1 issue?*

The current $250 value of this magazine is mostly based on having the 1954 Topps baseball card foldout intact.

Baseball Memorabilia

*The first issue of **Sports Illustrated** had a baseball card foldout. Wasn't there another issue with cards, too? Does it have any value?*

There were four early SI issues with baseball card foldouts. They are printed on regular paper, not cardboard. The Aug. 16, 1954, premiere issue of SI has a gatefold reproducing 1954 Topps cards. The next week's issue has a foldout of several 1954 Topps New York Yankee cards in full color and some 1954-style Yankees cards in black-and-white. It is much scarcer than the first issue, but sells for about 25-50 percent less. Even rarer are the two SIs that had foldouts reproducing 1955 Topps cards. They can be found in the April 11, 1955, and April 18, 1955, issues.

*Which issue of **Life** magazine carried sample Post cereal cards of Mickey Mantle and Roger Maris?*

April 13, 1962.

*I purchased a April 30, 1951, **Life** magazine, Vol. 30, No. 18. On pages 104-106 is a story on Mickey Mantle, called "Mickey Makes It." Does this magazine have any value?*

Yes, some, but not as much as it would be if Mantle were on the cover. Depending on its condition, the magazine could be worth as much as $10.

*I have some 1970-1972 issues of **The Sporting News**. Some of the covers include Roberto Clemente, Willie Mays, Pete Rose and Reggie Jackson. Are they valuable?*

Because of their size, and the fact they were printed on newsprint which yellows with age, old issues of TSN are not in great demand by collectors. You might find a superstar collector who has been seeking a particular cover, and would pay $10 or so for it, but a typical price is closer to $ 3-$5 for that era.

*I bought several 1978 **Dynamite** magazines (issue #47). Inside was a panel of six Topps baseball cards, supposedly cut from a regular Topps sheet of that year. I have some that have a duplication of players — one card on top of the other — such as Sal Bando, Tony Perez and Graig Nettles. Why?*

Because that's the way Topps configured its press sheets in the late-1970s and early-1980s. Most years had a number of cards double-printed, to help fill out the 132-card sheets. Naturally those cards are twice as common as the rest of the cards on the sheet. The double-prints in those years are quite often star players.

*I'm thinking of putting the attractive covers of **Baseball Cards** in a nonremovable plastic covering. Will this decrease the collectible value of them?*

We do not recommend laminating in plastic any type of collectible. Pocket plastic sheets large enough to hold an issue of *Baseball Cards* and other magazines are available. Why not buy a handful of them?

*I have **Baseball Cards** magazines from the Spring 1983 issue through the March 1991 issue. I would like to know where I can find the value of the issues and the cards in them.*

Since there is no price guide for hobby magazines, their value (and that of their insert cards) is subject to negotiation between buyer and seller. We've seen dealers selling back issues with the cards intact for between $5-$25, depending on the cards inside.

*Is it better to keep **Sporting News** magazines intact? There are some good photos of baseball players. Should I cut them out?*

If you cut the photos out, they will have absolutely no collector value. However, since modern issues of TSN have no collector value, either, enjoy the player photos any way you wish.

Glasses, Bottles & Cans

I have a water glass I put away in the 1950s with Joe DiMaggio painted in blue and "Joe DiMaggio's San Francisco" inscribed on it. Is it valuable?

Not particularly. DiMaggio owned a popular restaurant in San Francisco for many, many years, and thousands of these glasses were taken home as souvenirs. Even so (considering the Yankee Clipper's continuing popularity), we've seen the glasses being offered for up to $100.

I have plastic 7-Eleven cups, 5½" tall, that appear to have been issued in the 1970s. The football players include Bubba Smith, J.D. Hill and Ken Anderson, and the one baseball player is Don Kessinger. Any information would be helpful.

The cups were issued in 1972 and 1973, and were given away by the convenience store chain with the purchase of a soda or crushed-ice drink. Sixty different baseball cups, with player portraits and a brief biography, were made in 1972; in

1973, 20 more cups showing Hall of Fame Greats were added to the set. Kessinger appears only in the 1973 set. The football cups were issued about the same time. Common cups sell for about 25 cents when you can find them, although a cup of Pete Rose may bring as much as $5. The football cups are valued even lower.

I bought a Pete Rose glass that shows him with the Expos. Will it increase in value?

Yes. This was a fairly limited-edition of four Expos glasses. Because Rose played for less than a season with the Expos, we feel souvenirs of this sort stay in Canada and will be quite collectible in the future.

What can you tell me about a can that has Pete Rose pictured on it and is called "Pete" chocolate flavored beverage?

1) It tasted terrible. 2) It's a 1978 issue. 3) They can be found at card shows selling for $5 or less.

I have a commemorative Coca-Cola bottle which has a St. Louis Cardinals logo and shows the scores of each game of the 1982 World Series. Are these types of bottles rare?

Usually no more than 1,000-2,000 cases of these bottles are produced regionally. Your bottle has a value of $15 if unopened; $2 if opened. Hope you weren't thirsty.

I have four unopened Coke cans that picture players from the 1984 World Champion Detroit Tigers. The dealer I obtained these cans from said they were very rare and only issued in three counties in Michigan. Does that make them valuable?

Rarity alone does not make value; there has to be demand. Since pop cans picturing baseball players are not especially popular with collectors, I wouldn't look for these to have any great degree of value — maybe a few dollars apiece somewhere down the road. The Coke Tigers were of limited issue, but many area dealers bought them in quantity, so there is no shortage of them for collectors who want them. A tip: Open the cans from the bottom and drain and rinse them. Soda left in a can too long may eventually eat through the metal at the seam.

I have two RC Cola cans which have photos of Mark Fidrych and Thurman Munson on them. Can you give me some information on these items?

241

Baseball Memorabilia

RC Cola produced a 70-can set of baseball players in 1977, and a 100-can set in the next year.

My father and I have a box of two RC Cola cans. They are in a small blue box with a New York Mets emblem on it. One can is white with blue stripes that says "1986 N.L. Champs", and the other is blue with white stripes and says "1986 World Champs." How many of these boxes/cans were issued?

Local soda bottlers often produce commemorative cans or bottles for winning teams. Quantities produced usually range from 10,000 to 50,000, sometimes more, depending on the size of the distribution area. Your RC Cola cans come in on the high-end of the production scale. They are more valuable left unopened, in their box.

How can I keep a 1977 RC Cola can of Robin Yount from rusting, and how can I get the rust off that is already on it?

If the can is rusting from the inside because of the acid in the cola, there is nothing you can do that will not cost a lot more than the can is worth. Rust on the outside of the can can be removed with a variety of products, such as naval jelly or steel wool. Keep the can dry and you should have no additional rusting.

Baseball Photos & Posters

I have some 7⅞" by 9⅝" black-and-white pictures of Tommy Davis, Mickey Mantle, Lou Burdette, Roy Sievers and Stan Musial. Do you have any information on them?

The glove in the photos are a giveway. You have promotional items issued by Rawlings Sporting Goods in the 1960s. We don't know how many are in the set, or whether you can call them a set in the strictest terms, because they were issued over a period of several years and were just one of many promotional items issued by Rawlings. They are quite scarce, but because of their over-size nature, are not in particularly strong demand.

I have a Lipton Tea World Series poster that has the covers of programs from 1903-1982 pictured on it. How many were printed? How were they distributed? What is its value in Mint condition?

Baseball Memorabilia

There is almost never information on how many of any collectible item was produced. It doesn't matter much anyway, since the ratio of supply to demand is what makes an item valuable. The posters were available in a mail-in offer. They are worth in the area of $3-$5.

My uncle gave me a color 5" by 7" pin-up of Mickey Mantle, along with other players, such as Willie Mays, Hank Aaron and Brooks Robinson. He has a whole box full of them. Can you tell me anything about them?

The pin-ups were inserts in packs of 1967 Topps cards. There are 32 in the set. Most sell for less than a $1 in typical condition. The Mantle is priced at about $12.

I have four tin plates with color photos of baseball players from Wheaties cereal in 1952. They measure about 3" by 4". I have two plates of Stan Musial and one of each of Ralph Kiner and Phil Rizzuto. What other players are in the set?

George Kell is the other known player, quite a bit scarcer than the others. In nice, unrusted condition, these plates sell for $30 or more — up to $50 for Musial.

I have a moviebook (flip book) of Babe Ruth hitting a home run. Inside there are 24 photos of Ruth's home run swing. What year was this put out? How were they obtained?

We can only guess on the year — late 1920s to perhaps 1935. They were inserted in packages of cereal.

I have three viewmaster slides of ballplayers from the 1950s, such as Yogi Berra, Phil Rizzuto, Johnny Mize, Roy Campenella, etc. Are there more of these?

Not for another 25 years. This set of three reels was done in 1953. When sold with the original envelope and folder describing the players, it's a $50-$100 set. A few team sets were also done in the late-1970s and early-1980s. They are harder to find than the 1950s set.

Quite a few years ago, my father gave me a picture album containing Cincinnati Reds players, including Don Gross and Joe Nuxhall. The player photos were 5" by 7" black-and-white, and had a deckle edge. Can you give me more information?

This was a 1957 issue of the Sohio gasoline company. There were 18 photos in the set, acquired at the company's service stations. A similar issue that year featured the Cleveland Indians.

I would like to know how much a 1954 St. Louis Cardinals team photo, with names and autographs, would be worth? It says "Compliments of Anheuser-Busch." It's in fair condition.

Are the autographs real or facsimile autographs? If they're real, its value would depend on who signed it (Musial being the only significant signature). If the autographs are facsimiles — which is our guess — it's hard to give it a value of more than $10, especially considering its less-than-top condition.

I have black-and-white photos of early Wynn, Bob Lemon, Al Rosen, Larry Doby, Joe Gordon, Jess Flores, Ray Murray, Dale Mitchell, Bob Kennedy, Thurman Tucker and Sam Zoldak. Were these issued as a set?

You apparently have a partial set of Cleveland Indians team-issued photos from 1950. One name that's obviously missing is Bob Feller, but other players that seem to be missing are Luke Easter, Jim Hegan, Mike Garcia, Steve Gromek and Ray Boone.

I have a windowed envelope that has "Chicago White Sox 12 star Players" printed at the bottom. The 12 players pictured are Al Lopez, Gary Peters, Al Weis, Juan Pizarro, Don Buford, Mike Hershberger, Ron Hansen, Joe Cunningham, J.C Martin, Dave Nicholson, Floyd Robinson and Pete Ward. What are they?

You have a Big League Books picture pack. The packs were produced by the Jay Publishing Co., from 1958-1965. You have a pack from 1964. Our experts say 77 different White Sox pictures are known. Picture packs were also made for football teams. Despite their age, they're a fairly common sight at shows, and certainly not as popular a collectible as the contemporary baseball card sets.

Other Paper Items

Back in 1953-1954 I made a couple of scrapbooks of the Milwaukee Braves. Newspaper and magazine articles are in these books, along with a lot of newspaper pictures. Is there any value to these books?

Only sentimental value. Collectors don't seem interested in other people's scrapbooks — unless there are rare old baseball cards pasted inside.

I have baseball card wrappers from the 1980s. Are they worth something? Or am I just wasting my time saving them?

Since they don't take up much space, why not hang onto them? If everybody else gets discouraged because nobody is interested in 1980s wrappers and throws theirs away, then yours could be valuable someday.

I got a Wiffle ball, and the box has a picture of Rick Sutcliffe and facsimile autograph. Is it worth saving?

Anything that's cardboard with a ball player's picture on it seems to be worth saving. Actually, these sell for a couple of bucks apiece.

I recently became interested in collecting wrappers but am unable to find a price guide that lists them. Can you help? Can you also tell me what the grades "Fine" and "Prime" mean in reference to wrappers?

"Prime" is the finest possible condition for a wrapper that has actually been used on a pack. It has no imperfections other than the normal creases and wrinkles. A "Fine" wrapper can have up to a ¼ inch worth of tears on the edges, or a little dirt, gum residue or other staining. Because of the relatively small number of people who collect wrappers, there is no price guide available.

I have two tickets from a Chicago Cubs game in the 1930s. Is there any value to them?

Unattributable rain checks or ticket stubs have minimal value.

I recently bumped into Cubs announcer Jack Brickhouse in a bar in downtown Chicago. After talking about baseball, he gave me a deck of playing cards with pictures of current and former Cubs. I've asked a few dealers what they're worth and have not gotten a definite answer. Are they worth keeping? How scarce are they?

The cards are worth keeping if nothing more than a souvenir of having the opportunity to talk to baseball with a Hall-of-Fame-caliber announcer. As collectors' items, they have no great value. We see decks offered at shows for $10 or less.

I have some original cartoon drawings I received as a gift from Topps when I ordered sets back in the 1960s. They are cartoons used on the backs of the 1959-

1961 Topps cards. Does material like this have any value? How do I determine a price?

On unique items, the determination of value is an individual negotiation between buyer and seller. In our hobby, many collectors with items of this nature place them for sale in a mail-bid auction in *Sports Collectors Digest*. There, interested buyers can place a bid based on what the item is worth to them, and the seller can determine whether the top bid is suitable.

As you are well aware, the 1953 Topps cards were produced from small oil paintings of the players. I have the painting that was used to produce the Bill Glynn card (#171). I'm quite sure this is a rare item. Can you give me an approximate value?

In a major New York auction in 1989, the original paintings used to produce the cards of some of the top players in the 1953 Topps set were sold for outrageous money. The Mickey Mantle painting brought $125,000. Willie Mays went for $88,000, Jackie Robinson for $71,000, Roy Campanella for $61,500, Whitey Ford for $35,000 and Bob Feller for $33,000. Today, however, these pieces would bring only a fraction of that money. Common players, such as Glynn, might be expected to retail in the area of $350 to $750.

My father bought me a 1988 Denver Broncos Super Bowl Champions Wheaties box. It doesn't contain cereal because it was never folded into a box. What can you tell me about this box? How many weren't destroyed?

There's no way to know how many of these were snuck out the back door of the printer. They sell at card shows around the country for $20 or so. Boxes of the 1987-1988 National Basketball Association runners-up, Detroit Pistons, have also been seen.

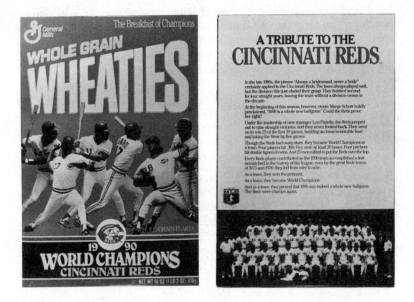

I have several Wheaties boxes with the pictures and a tribute to the 1990 World Champion Cincinnati Reds. Are the boxes worth more if they are unopened and full?

Yes, but only if you have a place to store them where the contents won't attract vermin who will chew through the box to get the cereal.

I have some Wheaties boxes with Pete Rose on the front. Do these have good potential value?

That's a good word for it — potential. Despite the fact the boxes are attractive and that Wheaties has a long history as an issuer of baseball collectibles, the Rose boxes have two strikes going against them: One, everybody saved them. Two, they are bulky to display and store. Our advice ... since you need boxes to store your other goodies in anyway, use the Wheaties boxes for storage. When full, put them in a poly bag to avoid scuffing the printed surface.

There are folders that resemble 1988 and 1989 Topps baseball cards. Will they be worth anything in the future?

Since they are an official Topps-licensed issue, we predict that they will have continued collector value in the future.

My uncle has in his collection some items called "Baseball Bucks." They look like money. He has a $10 Stan Musial. Who made these?

"Baseball Bucks" were issued in their own 1-cent packs by Topps in 1962. There are 96 individual "bucks" in the set, each measuring 4⅛" by 1¾". A complete set of Baseball Bucks in Near-Mint condition is valued at $650. A Musial sells in the $30 range.

I have a 1925 official National League baseball schedule put out by "The Gazette Times." It was printed on a celluloid card, 2" by 3". I would like to know if it is worth anything.

Not much. Unless an item like this pictures an actual player, or has a team logo, it has little collector value. It may be scarce, but the only thing scarcer is a potential buyer.

I recently bought about 50 matchbook cover baseball cards for $10 at a flea market. There were only three players I ever heard of — Dizzy Dean, Frankie Frisch and Handy Gowdy. Are they rare? Were they worth the $10 I paid for them?

Matchbook covers with player photos were the phenomenon of the 1930s. In all, nearly 1,100 different covers are known in six basic series. They are quite scarce today, but not popular with collectors, so prices are not high. At 20-cents each, you made a good deal.

I acquired some matchbook covers, apparently of the early 1930s, which have pictures of baseball players, pro and college football players, and pro hockey players. I've checked with a couple of the top dealers for information on these and received only vague answers. Can you give me any information on them?

In the early 1930s, there were more than a half a dozen major series — up to 200 players in each — of matchbook covers issued covering the sports you describe, as well as many smaller issues. In addition, many of the sets were issued with several different backgrounds. The best checklist of these items is found in the early editions of the *Sports Collectors Bible.* For better or worse, few people actively collect these, so they generally carry very reasonable price tags.

Baseball Statues and Figurals

I have a ceramic bank that has Chief Wahoo from the Cleveland Indians. Wahoo is leaning on a baseball bat. On the bottom of the bank are the words "Stanford Pottery Sebring." Does this have any value?

There is no set retail value for unique items like you have. They can range from $5-$50 or more. I suggest you attempt to locate a sports memorabilia dealer in the Cleveland area for an opinion. Another option is to place a mail-bid auction ad in an issue of *Sports Collectors Digest.* That way, you let the bidders determine a fair value.

I have a seven-inch tall Mickey Mantle plastic doll with a white Yankees uniform. He is in a batting stance but the bat is missing. What year and company was this made by, and what is it worth?

This is one of 18 baseball players in a series known to collectors as Hartland Statues. They were made in the late 1950s and early 1960s. With the bat missing, value of the Mantle Hartland, one of the more common, is less than $50. Origi-

nal replacement bats can be purchased from dealers for $10-$15.

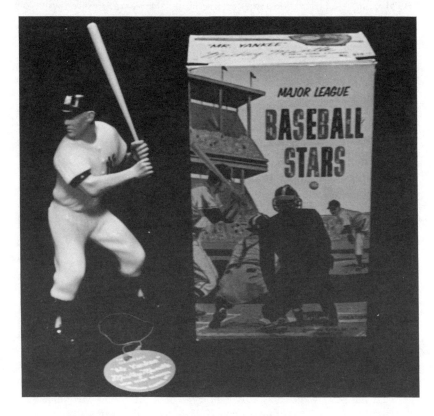

Do you think a 25th anniversary Mickey Mantle Hartland will be worth the same as the original in the future?

There will always be more demand for the original, so that price will remain higher.

Baseball Memorabilia

My grandfather was digging through his attic and came across an old Stan Musial plastic statue, showing him in a batting follow-through. I haven't been able to find any information on it. It is 2½" tall and has a name plate at the bottom. It has no copyright or other information on it.

Your statue is from an early-1950s issue by Dairy Queen. We recently saw the Musial statue advertised for $40.

A friend of mine recently gave my son six boxes of Trans-0-Gram miniature baseball statues of the 1969 Amazing Mets. On the back of the boxes are cards of the players. Can you tell me more about these?

According to the *SCD Baseball Card Price Guide,* the Trans-0-Gram Mets statues were the third in a series produced in 1969-1970. There was a 60-player all-star set in 1969, a 30-player all-star set in 1970, and the 15-player Mets set in 1970. Complete boxes with statues are the most valuable way to save these collectibles. Single cards cut from boxes and loose statues are worth less.

Do you have any information on ceramic dolls whose heads bob? On the bottom of the statue is written "Exclusive License Rights 1962."

What you have is known as a "bobbin' head doll." Such dolls were made in Japan from 1960-1972, sold for around $2.95, and usually portrayed team mascots, either "figurals" — animals, birds or whatever for the Tigers, Cubs, Reds, Braves, Indians, Colt .45s, Cardinals and Orioles — or chubby kiddie figures, in that team's uniform.

Dolls of real players are scarcer. They were made for Mickey Mantle, Henry Aaron, Willie Mays, Roberto Clemente and Roger Maris. Although the Maris

252

doll is scarce and some of the Mays variations are super-scarce, the Mantle doll is among the five most valuable in the hobby. The Clemente is the most valuable. Mantle and Maris dolls came in their own personalized boxes, which are valuable in and of themselves.

With bobbin' head dolls, as with any collectible, value is based on condition. Many bobbin' head dolls regularly sell for more than $100.

I collect Starting Lineup figures. Are they worth any money? Are they worth more unopened?

There is a small, but fanatical, group of collectors pursuing the Starting Lineup figures in all their many variations. Some sell for more than $50 already. They are definitely worth more money in the original packaging.

Are the Kenner baseball statues being distributed only in their respective team areas? I have been unable to locate West Coast players here on the East Coast.

Generally speaking, the Kenner statues are only found in retail outlets around the player's home team area. This has created quite a demand for trading partners around the country.

Miscellaneous Items

I have a child's uniform and jacket of the Milwaukee Braves dating back to the early 1960s. Do these items have any collector value? If so, where can I find out how much?

Virtually every souvenir item issued for a baseball team — especially a defunct baseball team — prior to the 1980s, has collector value. Unfortunately, there is no price guide for items like these. You'd have to offer the items via a mail auction or shop them around to a number of dealers and collectors at a show to get an idea of their worth. We'd estimate the items might be $25-$50 each, in decent condition.

Are World Series hats and pennants worth anything?

Are your memories worth anything? Recent pennants and hats are usually worth more for their sentimental value than they are as collectibles. There are exceptions, but don't invest in them thinking they'll rocket upward in value. It just won't happen.

I have two bats that were passed down to me from a great uncle who played pro ball in the 1930s. They are black and have inscribed "Brooklyn Dodgers National League Champions," and the dates 1947 and 1949. They also have the names of the players in gold lettering. I'd like to know how many bats were produced for each year.

Like most baseball collectibles, there is no way to know how many were originally produced. These World Series black bats were issued by the teams as souvenirs to players, staff and, in many cases, officials at the minor league levels. Thus, while of limited issue, it must be assumed there were two or three hundred of each distributed. Fortunately for you, the Dodgers World Series bats are among the most popular and in demand. In decent condition, value would start at $300.

I have a Ted Williams model bat from the mid-1950s. It is a No. 9 model bat and was made by Hillerich & Bradsby Co., of Louisville. Please give me an idea of how much this bat is worth.

In unused condition, store-model bats of superstars of the 1950s can sell for $20-$70 or so, but buyers are scarce.

Right before the demise of the Oakland Invaders, I obtained two of the team helmets. I have since learned all the others were sold to a college back East, stripped of their logos and repainted. Is there value in these one-of-a-kind items?

Among football collectors, the memorabilia of the USFL is quite popular. Helmets are always in strong demand by collectors.

What can you tell me about these small (2¾" by 6") player pennants?

Baseball Memorabilia

Issued about 1916 as a candy premium, there are nearly 100 different players known, with several colors of felt pennants for some of the players. They are not as popular with collectors as contemporary card issues because of their odd size. In top grade they range in value from $25 for commons to more than $300 to Ty Cobb and Joe Jackson.

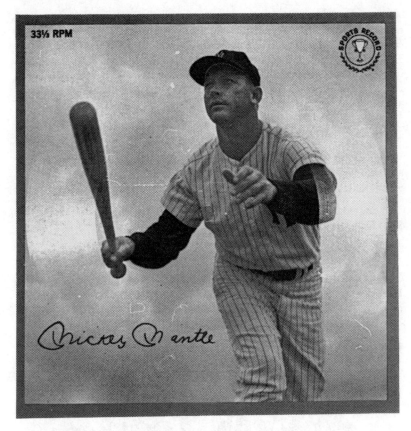

I have some baseball player records marked "Sports Champions, Inc., 1962. Aurovision, a product of Columbia records." Do you have any information on these?

These color photo records were issued in 1962 and again in 1964 — you can tell which year from the stats on the back. There were 20 in the 1962 set and 16 in the 1964 set. It seems a hoard of them has come onto the market; we've seen the complete sets being offered for as low as $100.

I saw a colorful metal sign for "Ted Williams Root Beer" at a flea market in perfect condition. Is it valuable?

Only if you like modern reproductions. There are also fantasy Williams root

beer bottles and mirrors to be found. They have no value as sports collectibles.

I have a pencil clip of Tom Byrne of the St. Louis Browns. I was wondering if it is rare.

These pencil clips were made between 1948-1952 and can be found with either St. Louis Browns or Cleveland Indians players on them. They are quite scarce, but, except for a few Hall of Famers to be found, are not particularly valuable, with common players retailing for $15 or so.

One of my students brought in an old brass ring. It is shaped like a baseball, has wheels to score balls, strikes and outs, and has an engraved autograph of Andy Pafko. We figured out it is an umpire's scorekeeping device, but what I want to know is if there are other players' names that can be found on them?

We've only seen this item with Pafko's name.

I am trying to obtain copies of back issues of your Baseball Cards Price Guide magazine that contain reprints of the 1957 Topps collector cards. Can you help?

We don't sell back issues. The issues you seek are dated from January 1990 through December 1990. They don't have reprints of Topps 1957 cards, but rather mini price guide cards of current players done in the style of the 1957 Topps. You'll occasionally find back issues of the magazines offered by our advertisers. Also, check your local card shops and shows. Expect to pay a minimum of $5 per issue. The November 1990 issue, with Michael Jordan on the cover, sells for $20 or more.

Investing
in Baseball Cards

Chapter Eleven

I'd like to invest in baseball cards. What would you suggest?

If you're interested in investing in baseball cards, then you had better start learning all you can about the hobby. It's not as simple as buying cards, sitting on them, then cashing them in for your retirement or child's college education. The business of baseball cards is a complex business, indeed. We suggest you talk to knowledgeable collectors and dealers to get their thoughts as to what has the greatest potential to increase in value. We'd also suggest you subscribe to one or more baseball publications mentioned in this book, as well as attending baseball card shows. You'll get a better feel for the baseball card market and future trends. Knowledge of the game of baseball and the players can also be of great benefit.

This type of basic preparation only makes sense. If you were to invest money in the stock market, you wouldn't just pick out any old stock. You'd either research the companies you were thinking about investing in or seek the advice of a stock broker on which stocks to buy. You'd also find out basically how the stock market works — some of the ins and outs of the business. Basically, investing in baseball cards is not that much different from investing in the stock market (though we believe it's a lot more fun).

And don't forget that any investment "advice" you receive, no matter what the source (including this book), is just opinions, not hard and fast rules. If you plan on investing in cards, we suggest you follow the steps as outlined in the opening paragraph, then make your own decisions on investment plans.

What cards do you expect to go up in value over the next few years?

This is a very difficult question to answer because the baseball card market changes on a daily basis. Specific baseball card investment advice is out of the scope of this book. For specific advice, consult the publications listed at the end of the "General Information" section. They often carry that kind of information.

What we can offer you here are general guidelines on cards that have proven solid investments over the past decade and which we expect to continue rising through the 1990s. They include tobacco and candy cards, top-grade complete sets from the 1930s through 1980, top-grade rookie and superstar cards before 1980, and unopened material (wax, rack and cello boxes and cases). Obviously, this list includes an enormous amount of material, and some items are better investments than others. With this huge amount of material and an ever-changing market, the successful baseball card investor does his homework and stays attuned to the trends in the hobby.

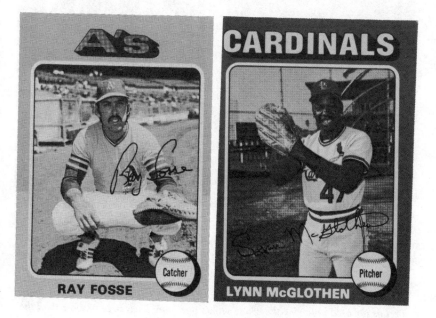

What's the difference between investing and speculating in baseball cards?

Basically, the difference is putting money into a proven commodity (investment) versus an unproven commodity (speculation). Generally, the newer the cards, the bigger the speculation, and conversely, the older the cards, the better the investment. The reasons behind this are supply and demand. Fewer cards were printed before 1980 than were printed after 1980. Also, relatively few pre-1980 cards remain today in top grade (Near Mint or better condition), while there are literally thousands of cards and sets after 1980 in top grade.

Simply put, buying a 1975 Topps set in Near Mint condition is an investment, while buying 100 cards of the newest hottest rookie on the market is a speculation. Speculation is a risky proposition.

Take, for example, the now-famous 1989 Fleer Billy Ripken card which contained an obscenity. Within weeks of its discovery, the cards was trading at $100

Investing in Baseball Cards

and more. Those who bought the card when it was at that level, and hung on to it, made a very costly speculation on a card which, in 1990, was valued from $20-$25. In 1991 it dropped to $18. However, speculating on cards can be exciting and profitable. At the beginning of 1989, you could have purchased thousands of 1987 Fleer Will Clark rookie cards at $2-$3 each. Just 12 months later, that card was valued at $35. You can figure yourself the type of profits on the Clark card had you stuck $100 in the cards at the start of 1989. But more often than not, the speculative baseball card market produces a Billy Ripken rather than a Will Clark.

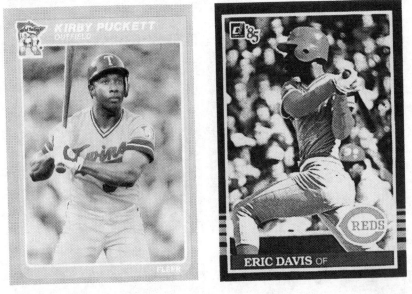

Strictly on an investment basis, would it be better to have one valuable card from a set as opposed to having the whole set? Is one more likely to appreciate than the other?

If you're talking about the most expensive card of a current set, the complete set is the best investment. Take the 1986 Donruss set, for example. The Jose Canseco card sold for $90 in 1991; a whole set sold for $200. If Canseco never has another good year, the value of his card will drop, but the value of the other 659 cards in the set is rising. Buying a set is an investment. Buying a single player's card is speculation.

As a novice in baseball cards, my biggest curiosity is this: As the hobby grows and many people, both young and old, buy full sets each year, what causes even the recent years' cards to increase in value at the surprising rate I have seen? Can I expect this to continue as more and more cards are printed, apparently with no limits?

Like any other collectible, the value of baseball cards is dependent on supply and demand. Much of the current upward price movement in recent (1981-date) cards is based on anticipated, rather than current, demand. Persons are speculating in hot stars and rookie cards with the expectation that when they try to sell, the increased number of collectors they believe will be on the market will have created a demand for those cards.

There is a big potential problem with that theory. Currently, Topps prints at least two million of each of its regular baseball cards. Yet, it's more likely there are fewer than two million persons who could be classified as serious enough collectors who would pay more than wax-pack price for a baseball card. If we assume the collector is the ultimate customer for all these cards now held by investors and speculators, it seems there is going to be a real shortage of real customers.

During good economic conditions in this country, there is a lot of disposable income around to buy and hold cards. If the economy were to take a downturn, however, as happened in the early-1980s, we might see a lot of recent cards being dumped on the market at a fraction of their current value. In short, speculating on baseball cards can be just as risky as buying pork belly futures or penny stocks.

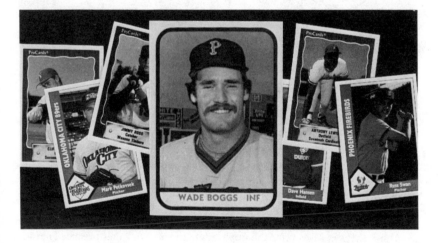

Are minor league cards a good investment?

Again, similar to major league cards, fewer minor league cards were printed before 1985 than after. We feel the older minor league team sets that contain superstar players, such as the 1981 Pawtucket set with Wade Boggs, will hold their value in the long run. As for the more recent sets, their future is only speculative now, although the strength of this segment of the hobby appears to be growing, with about four companies producing minor league sets at this time.

One thing to remember about minor league cards is to buy them in complete team sets only — never individually. Serious minor league hobbyists and dealers buy, sell and trade in complete team sets only.

261

Could you tell me, as far as increase in value, if it is better to collect complete Mint sets of say 1989 Topps, or unopened wax pack cases of 1989 Topps?

We'd opt for the wax cases (and rack and cello cases) for three reasons. First, they have historically been a better investment because few people could afford to put them away. That, however, has changed somewhat in recent years, and there are many, many garages and attics full of recent wax cases waiting for prices to rise. Those hordes could keep prices from rising too far too fast on cards from, say, 1986 to date.

Second, if you have wax cases, and for some reason set prices start going through the roof, you always have the option of opening the packs and making sets.

Third, the wax cases offer the opportunity to vary your unit of sale. That is, you can sell the whole case, or you can sell individual boxes or single packs.

For appreciation, should I invest in a regular Mint set of Topps for a given year, or a glossy set of Topps for that year?

We give the edge to the Tiffany (glossy) for long-term appreciation, when people find out how relatively scarce they are. In the short-term, however, it's a toss-up. Assume you have $100 to spend on the current year's Topps set. You could purchase four regular sets or one Tiffany set. And when the price of the regular set doubles, you'd have four $50 sets, or one $200 set — no difference.

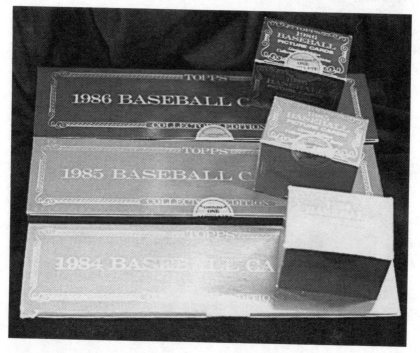

Tiffany sets (or Fleer Glossy sets) haven't really caught on with collectors yet, but we feel someday demand will increase.

What affect do card grades have on investing in cards? Also, what kind of card grades should I be looking at as far as getting the most for my investment dollar?

History has shown that the top-grade cards have appreciated most rapidly in the hobby, so top-grade cards are a must for investors.

Specifically, if you're buying cards from 1980-present, don't settle for any cards in less than Mint condition. With cards from the 1970s, stay at Near Mint condition or better, and with cards prior to 1970, the lowest grade you'd want is Excellent to Excellent-Mint; Near Mint is better, and Mint better still (although extremely difficult to locate).

One piece of advice — don't make any major purchase until you know how to properly grade cards. To an untrained eye, a Near Mint and Excellent card may look the same, although in reality they can be tens, hundreds or even thousands of dollars apart.

What do you think about investing in Traded or Update sets?

These post-season sets have proven to be very popular with collectors since Topps introduced them in 1981. And with few exceptions, all have appreciated

nicely in value over the years. One reason is the sets contain a large number of "first cards" of players, such as the 1983 Topps Traded Darryl Strawberry, which was valued at $110 in 1991. Another reason these sets are in demand is because they are produced in lesser numbers than the regular sets. Demand and a lesser quantity has made these sets a good investment in the 1980s, and we expect them to continue their popularity in the 1990s.

What are the prospects on the 1990 Philadelphia Chewing Gum Co. "Swell" baseball greats?

If you mean the prospects that a lot of collectors will enjoy seeing their old heroes on new cards, the prospects are excellent. If you mean the prospects that these cards will increase in value, the prospects are unlikely.

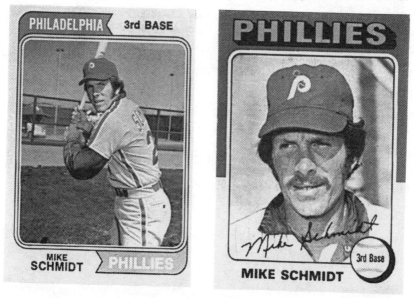

Mike Schmidt will be elected to the Hall of fame in a few years. Would his cards be a good investment?

Yes. Cards of players who will be elected to the Hall of Fame get a boost from collectors. Usually, the most appreciation occurs just after the player announces his retirement, and the two years prior to the player taking his spot in Cooperstown. The cards of a popular home-run hitter such as Schmidt should rise in value appreciably in the years prior to his Hall of Fame voting time.

Because of all Pete Rose's problems, will his cards ever be popular again?

The future value of Rose cards hinges on whether he will be elected to the Hall of Fame. At this point, that event is uncertain. If not elected, his cards would probably not see much movement — either up or down. But if elected, his cards would rise. We believe Rose will be elected to the Hall of Fame at some point, but there are just as many (probably more) who feel he won't be, thus we would classify Rose cards as a speculation.

How come all of Rickey Henderson's cards are going down?

Although he is the best leadoff hitter in baseball and holds the all-time stolen base record, Henderson is not all that popular with fans and collectors. Many perceive him to be an arrogant, cry-baby hotdog. Prices are going down because the supply of his cards exceeds current demand.

I have 1990 Topps cello pack with Jerome Walton and Deion Sanders on the top. Will they be as valuable as past cello packs even though it's harder to see the players?

Investing in Baseball Cards

We feel the 1990 cellos of all companies will never become as valuable as earlier packs for two reasons: 1) Topps, Fleer and Donruss have all gone to the type of packaging that makes it nearly impossible to see the top card. This makes the 1990 cellos much less attractive as display pieces than earlier issues. 2) With the recent publicity on how scarce valuable racks and cellos are with stars and rookies showing, many more of them are now being saved.

Are unopened rack and cello packs with stars and rookies showing a good investment?

These types of items have a lot of things going for them, the first of which is they make great-looking and unique display pieces. Second, considering that cards in the 1980s have been bought and sold in the millions, unopened packs with stars/rookies are very rare — they're not impossible to find, but very rare in comparison to single cards. Value for an unopened pack with a star/rookie showing on top is about two to three times the value of the card showing, so if the card has a $5 value, the pack should sell for about $15. Packs with stars on the bottom are not as highly collected as those with the star on top; their values and investment potential are accordingly lower.

266

Do you think investing in ceramic baseball player statues and other sports art is a wise decision?

It would seem so. For example, a Don Mattingly statue, which was issued a few years ago for around $125, has been trading on the secondary market for more than $600. Some baseball stadium lithographs have also risen appreciably. The key to these kinds of items increasing in value is quality and a limited issue number.

Investing in Baseball Cards

Is the 1991 Topps Stadium Club set a good investment?

Not now. It was in the early stages at low prices, but the price for wax packs rose so fast it lessened the long-term investment potential. Buyers had to spend too much too fast to invest in the cards. The 600-card set, issues in two series, has a value of $250.

Price guides don't list the 1991 Topps Micro sets. Could you tell me the potential value of an unopened complete set?

If we could, we wouldn't have to publish magazines for a living. Future value of this set — like every other sports collectible — will be determined by supply and demand. We like the investment potential of the set because it can currently be bought at or below what the dealers originally paid, yet there are not a lot of the sets to be found. It's an idea that's not likely to be repeated, and someday superstar collectors will realize they want the micro versions of 1991 Topps cards.

I recently bought a pack of 1991 Upper Deck baseball. On the very top was the Michael Jordan special insert card. I've read this card is scarce, but when I go into baseball card shops they have stacks of the card. How many of these cards were made? Is it a good investment?

Upper Deck doesn't release production figures, so we have no way of knowing how many were produced. The price of this novelty card has been falling fast. It used to retail for up to $20, but now you can find it everywhere for $10. We feel the price will continue to drift downward for the forseeable future.

1992 Card Issues

1992 Donruss

1992 Classic

1992 Donruss

1992 Score

1992 Fleer

1992 Score

1992 Topps

1992 Upper Deck

1992 Topps

Pinpoint the value of your collection.

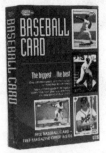

Standard Catalog of Baseball Cards
3rd edition
800 pages approx., 8-1/2" x 11"

Featuring current values for more than 135,000 cards, this massive book is the most comprehensive price guide the hobby has ever seen. Includes cards from all manufacturers and all eras. Often referred to as the "bible of the hobby"................$29.95

SCD Baseball Card Price Guide
6th edition
736 pages, 6" x 9"
The largest, most authoritative price guide ever published for baseball cards produced since 1948. All together, you'll find more than 75,000 cards and over 225,000 prices. Considered by many to be the single best buy in a baseball card price guide......$13.95

Krause covers the bases

SPORTS COLLECTORS DIGEST

The only weekly publication for advanced collectors of sportscards and related memorabilia. Packed with plenty of hobby news, player features, card prices plus ads for thousands of cards and collectibles.

52 weekly issues $49.95

CARD NEWS

Comprehensive, bi-weekly coverage of cards and collectibles for baseball, football, basketball, hockey and other sports. Each issue features hobby updates, articles, card prices, ads for cards and memorabilia and more.

26 bi-weekly issues $26.95

BASEBALL CARDS

Monthly magazine filled with news, player profiles, baseball card prices, collecting and investing tips, baseball card prices, ads and free collector's edition repli-cards. Terrific reading for collectors of all ages.

12 monthly issues $18.95

SPORTS CARD PRICE GUIDE

The hobby's most accurate monthly price guide for baseball, football, basketball and hockey cards from all major card manufacturers. Also included are collecting tips, investment advice, buy and sell opportunities and 8 free repli-cards in each big issue.

12 monthly issues $18.95

Return with payment to:
**Krause Publications
Sports Circulation Dept.
700 E. State St.
Iola, WI 54990-0001**

**MasterCard & VISA cardholders
save time by calling toll-free**

800-258-0929 Dept. 7QC

Mon.-Fri. 6:30 a.m.-8 p.m., CST
Sat. 8 a.m.-2 p.m., CST

Non-order callers, please use our regular business line: (715) 445-2214.

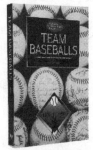